To Bob
With affection
and admiration

Steve
Shoemaker

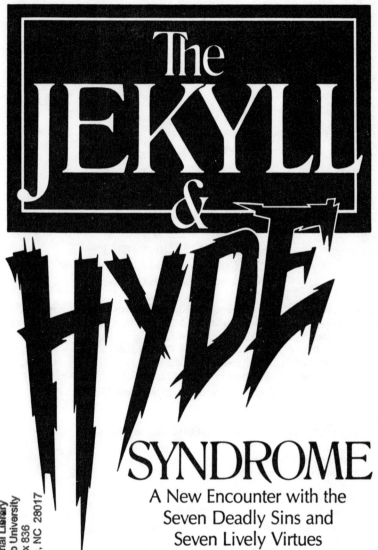

# The JEKYLL & HYDE SYNDROME

## A New Encounter with the Seven Deadly Sins and Seven Lively Virtues

### H. Stephen Shoemaker

**BROADMAN PRESS**
Nashville, Tennessee

© Copyright 1987 ● Broadman Press
All rights reserved
4215-38
ISBN: 0-8054-1538-6
Dewey Decimal Classification: 241
Subject Heading: CHRISTIAN ETHICS
Library of Congress Catalog Card Number: 86-28356
Printed in the United States of America

**Library of Congress Cataloging-in-Publication Data**

Shoemaker, H. Stephen, 1948
  The Jekyll and Hyde syndrome.

  Includes bibliographies.
  1. Deadly sins.   2. Virtues.   3. Theological
virtues.   4. Christian ethics—Baptist authors.
I. Title.
BV4626.S47   1987      241'.3      86-28356
ISBN 0-8054-1538-6

To Cherrie Shoemaker who embodies
the *hesed* of God in our
covenant relationship.

# Foreword by
# Wayne E. Oates

Sin and virtue have become inarticulate realities with which the average person today struggles in lonely isolation. He or she does not speak of them. To speak of them is to appear either more unsophisticated or religious than is the "socially appropriate" thing to do. It is not "trendy" if one values sophistication. It is to appear uncouth at best and, at worst, to appear unsaved to speak too much of sin and virtue in conventional religious company. In fact, to confess the presence of sin or a conviction of a virtue may even invite the "diagnosis" of being a wee bit mentally disturbed! Such is the hunger for appearances which permeates the conversation of most gatherings today. Yet, this is not totally true. To do so, however, one must be a part of one of the many "anonymous" life-support groups such as Alcoholics Anonymous, Gamblers Anonymous, or a psychotherapeutic group. Stephen Shoemaker relieves you and me of such shame.

In the face of this seemingly benevolent conspiracy of silence, Stephen Shoemaker has broken with the hush-hushness of a people who ask whatever happened to sin. He has brought catalogs of sins and recitals of virtues into vivid and unforgettable words. He has in this book done what each of us yearns that his or her pastor would do. He has put into words things we have felt but have been without anything but a cry to express. We may have dared to converse with our spouse, a close friend, or a counselor whom we see only in the anonymity and privacy of a consulting room. Yet when we have gone to church we either have not had such an opportunity or felt it would not be appropriate to divulge our feelings. Now, right before our eyes on the pages of this book our thoughts have been framed into plain speech by a Christian pastor.

Therefore, as you read these pages, you are brought into conversation with wisdom, spiritual direction, and deep compassion concerning your besetting sins and temptations. You are affirmed in your deepest spiritual strivings for the Christ-given strengths usually spoken of as virtues. You are not only met in your darkest dilemmas, you are informed with the depths of scriptural knowledge. You are directed by a "person of understanding" into the paths of wisdom, courage, justice, and temperance through the power of the faith, hope, and love that being crucified with Christ resurrects in us who have been raised to walk in the newness of life. Whether you are a new Christian or a veteran in the way of Christ, Stephen Shoemaker's firm but affectionate encounter of your sins and your virtues will be as it has been to me in my own sins and virtues—edifying. He does not tear down; he builds up.

As he does so, he brings things both old and new from the Scripture and Christian history, on the one hand, and from contemporary psychological and psychiatric understandings of human nature. These are carefully written essays of great substance. Yet they have stood the test of week-by-week preaching with elaborate feedback from a great congregation. You and I as readers are benefited by not only the leadership of Stephen Shoemaker but also by this "pre-testing" of his thought. Yet, you and I are not simply overhearing sermons he has preached to a congregation. We are an audience in our own right and he speaks the word of the Lord to us afresh in these pages. When you have finished the last chapter, I think you will do as I have done; you will thank God and take heart in your spiritual journey.

WAYNE E. OATES
Professor of Psychiatry and Behavioral Sciences
School of Medicine, University of Louisville
Senior Professor, Psychology of Religion
The Southern Baptist Theological Seminary
Louisville, Kentucky
September 28, 1986

# Preface and Acknowledgments

All words find their meaning within the living language of a community. What is sin? What is virtue? What do the seven sins and seven virtues look like? How do they behave? Reporters tell us that there are certain tribal languages that do not distinguish between green and blue and whose members have trouble telling the difference between the two colors. The problem is not physiological but linguistic. If you and I are morally discerning persons, it is because we have been taught a moral language in a morally intentional community. The Judeo-Christian heritage and the moral tradition of the West have made the seven sins and seven virtues part of the basic grammar of our life. And we are better for it.

The sins and virtues, then, take their shape within this moral tradition. More precisely, they find their meaning for me within the biblical story, a magnificent story which finds its beginning with creation, its moment of truth in the Christ event, and its fulfillment in the heavenly city of God. This is a book about morals, but these morals find their life within the larger moving picture of God's history with us. The foundational motifs of the story are biblical, but the story also includes the philosophical and intellectual traditions of the West. All truth is finally one. God is the author of all truth, and Jesus Christ as the Logos, the truth or word made flesh, is the one by whom all truth is judged.

You will see my debt to the Bible and to broad Western tradition represented by such persons as Aristotle, Augustine, Aquinas, Chaucer, and Freud. Contemporary thinkers have also made their mark: Reinhold Niebuhr, Dorothy Sayers, Willard Gaylin, and Henry Fairlie, whose book *The Seven Deadly Sins Today* got me started on this project.

I owe a deep debt of gratitude to the institutions of higher learning—Stetson University, Southeastern Baptist Theological Seminary, Union Theological Seminary, New York City, and The Southern Baptist Theological Seminary—that whetted my appetite for truth and taught me that the goal of learning is to make better persons and a better world. I thank Crescent Hill Baptist Church who heard me talk about sins and virtues and talked back, and who gave me a summer sabbatical so I could study at Oxford where I began my study of virtue. (I didn't need a sabbatical to learn about sin.) I also thank Cherie Williams, a parishioner and friend, who typed the manuscript and gave good advice.

I wish to thank Nancy Elizabeth Foil for the calligraphy which introduces each chapter. Now serving as a staff minister of Baptist Temple Church, Alexandria, Virginia, she is an artist whose calligraphy itself is an art form.

Finally, I thank Cherrie Shoemaker, my wife, to whom this book is lovingly dedicated.

# Contents

# Introduction

Growing up I remembered *Dr. Jekyll and Mr. Hyde* as a particularly horrifying monster movie: The good Dr. Jekyll turned into a monstrous evil being. Upon reading Robert Louis Stevenson's novel *Dr. Jekyll and Mr. Hyde* as an adult, I rediscovered it as a psychological and spiritual thriller—a tale of two natures if you will, a morality play which on its surface is a horror story but on a deeper level is a story about the age-old human dilemma: the human struggle between good and evil. It is almost as if we have not one nature but two—a good and an evil nature which are in conflict.

Dr. Jekyll was an upright gentleman raised in Victorian England with a strict sense of right and wrong. The problem was that good Dr. Jekyll was tormented by evil impulses which he sometimes secretly indulged. He could not be happy as a good man because of the pull of these evil impulses; neither could he be happy as an evil man because of his active conscience that plagued him with guilt. In his own words, Dr. Jekyll had "a perennial war among my members."[1]

As the plot went, Dr. Jekyll tried a chemical solution to his dilemma. By drinking a certain potion he sought to separate the good and evil natures. He became two separate and different persons—good Dr. Jekyll and evil Mr. Hyde. He theorized:

If each, I told myself, could be housed in separate identities, life would be relieved of all that was unbearable; the unjust might go his way, delivered from the aspirations and remorse of his more upright twin; and the just could walk steadfastly and securely on his upward path . . . no longer exposed to the disgrace and penitence by the hands of this extraneous evil.[2]

Don't you wish it could be so easily solved? If only we could push a button or drink a potion and be two separate persons. We could one day be good with no pull of temptation and the next day indulge the darker, wilder side with no twinge of guilt and no injury to our good self. Dr. Jekyll's experiment failed, however, as do all our attempts to deal superficially with the two natures. He lost control of when he would be Jekyll and when Hyde. Evil Mr. Hyde would unexpectedly and intrusively take over Dr. Jekyll.

How are we to deal with the dual nature, or as I would prefer to express it, with the self's battle between good and evil? The Genesis account of creation tells us that when God made us, He called us "good." We are not an evil self nor are we two selves— one evil and one good—competing for supremacy. We are one good self susceptible to the presence and power of evil and free to choose whether to be the good self God created us to be or to become enthralled with evil and give ourselves over to it. What we feel or experience as a battle between two inner selves is in reality the one true self seeking to determine who we are and whose we are. So again I put the question: How are we to deal with the battle between good and evil? Enter the apostle Paul—a "soul brother" to Dr. Jekyll. Paul knew what it meant to have "warring members within." He called this inner tension the warfare between the old nature and the new nature, or between "spirit" and "flesh," and confessed his inner struggle in words Dr. Jekyll would find all too familiar: "I do not understand my own actions. . . . For I do not do the good I want, but the evil I do not want is what I do. Wretched man that I am! Who will deliver me from this body of death?" (Rom. 7:15, 19,24).

We can sympathize; the war goes on within us. It may even

be worse today than in post-Victorian America where the old notions of right and wrong are called into question. John Updike's characters are a poignant study of modern Americans wandering in a moral wilderness. One of his characters, Jerry Conant, in *Marry Me* says: "Maybe our trouble is that we live in the twilight of the old morality and there's just enough to torment us, and not enough to hold us in."[3]

What I am describing, whether from the teachings of the first-century apostle Paul or the characterizations of Robert Louis Stevenson's nineteenth-century Dr. Jekyll or Updike's modern American, Jerry Conant, is what I call the "Jekyll and Hyde Syndrome." The Jekyll and Hyde Syndrome describes the malaise of all who live in unresolved tension between good and evil. We continually feel the strain of the battle, never feeling victory over the pull of evil and too frequently falling prey to its lure. We are not happy being bad but cannot find any consistent ability to be good. We have tried any number of solutions to little avail; still the battle rages.

There are several superficial ways to deal with the conflict. One way is the path of *legalism.* The apostle Paul found this to be a most unsatisfactory method. Not only did the Law fail to control the evil side, it often fueled its fires the way forbidden fruit lures us in its forbiddenness. The Law puts the self in a straitjacket of rules, but sooner or later these rules fail to solve the dilemma. Legalism, the way of external restraint, does not work.

Another way is the path of *repression* or internal restraint. This was the premier Victorian solution. Guilt-ridden people were taught to drive their "evil" thoughts and feelings down into the unconscious. Repression does not work—at least not for long. Sigmund Freud helped us traverse the terrain of repression and neurosis, teaching us that repression cannot help us control our darker impulses. Instead, by repressing them we lose control over them.

Another way is the path of *indulgence.* A pop-Freudian overreaction to the problems of Victorian repression was to argue: You exorcise the demon of dark impulses by expressing them. Let it all hang out; do what "comes nat'urly" and you will be happy, healthy, and free, free from an immature notion of sin and the neurotic feeling of guilt. This solution argues from the supposition that feelings which are held in are unhealthy; therefore, the road to health is to express them. Such a position, says Willard Gaylin, noted psychoanalyst and philosopher, is based upon "a sloppy reading of early Freud."[4] It has, moreover, proved to be bad advice. Indulging the evil nature does not exhaust it, it revs it up for more!

Another solution to the dilemma is to pretend it does not exist, to do away with the moral categories of good and evil by adopting an *amoral secularism.* It is a laissez-faire attitude toward morality: No authority should dictate moral rules. This position says there is no such thing as good and evil; there is only healthy and unhealthy, the productive or unproductive, what works and what doesn't. Moral categories are replaced by psychological or pragmatic ones. No less than Harvard psychiatrist, Robert Coles, has taken on the educational establishment to say: "Replacing moral philosophy with psychology has been a disaster, an absolute disaster."

The Jekyll and Hyde Syndrome describes the person who lives in perpetual misery because the battle between good and evil rages on unresolved. Legalism, repression, indulgence, and secularism have not worked. Such a person is truly miserable. Constantly tempted to do wrong, he or she is unable to be happy being either good or bad. This person may maintain upright behavior but constantly battles darker impulses, or this person has indulged the darker side and now lives with a trail of damaged lives and relationships.

This book offers a way to escape the Jekyll and Hyde Syndrome. Its purpose is to help you strengthen your moral self in order to be both good and happy being good. Strengthening the moral self is developing the basic true and good self God made you to be. This path demands a new moral seriousness with which you approach life. This moral seriousness involves the use of these strategies: knowledge, behavioral change, laughter, and, most importantly, grace.

*Knowledge* is the enterprise by which we seek to know what is morally right. The Judeo-Christian tradition and Western philosophical tradition offer us much help here. To identify what is morally right is to set our feet on a higher path; and to identify what is sinful is to gain an upper hand. As the ancients said, to name the demon is to gain control of it.

*Behavioral change* is the enterprise by which we seek to do what is morally right. Any morally serious search commits itself to change in behavior from the beginning. How we behave will have an effect on how we feel and think.

*Laughter* is the enterprise by which we poke fun at our own humanity and at the tactics of the Evil One. Morality is much too serious to be solemn. Being able to laugh at yourself in your human foibles and frailty gives you the energy to keep on. And as for making fun of the Evil One, Martin Luther offers this advice: "The best way to drive out the devil, if he will not yield to texts of Scripture, is to jeer and flount him, for he cannot bear scorn."[5] C. S. Lewis's, *The Screwtape Letters,* is a masterpiece of such strategy.

*Grace* is the gift of God that comes in the twin forms of pardon and power.[6] As pardon, grace forgives our sin, cleanses us of evil, and heals our relationship to God, self, and neighbor. As power, grace delivers us from sin's grip and fills us with the power of new life, the power of goodness. Any final solution to the Jekyll and Hyde Syndrome comes as we receive the grace of God in our lives.

As a Christian, I confess that it has been Jesus Christ who has brought God's grace to me. In His life, death, and resurrection, He manifested God's grace *for* us. In His living Spirit, He dwells within us and offers God's grace *in* us. Jesus Christ is the secret to the solving of the Jekyll and Hyde Syndrome. His grace comes as pardon to save us from despair and guilt; His grace comes as power to strengthen our moral resolve and give us the power of goodness. We need both forms of grace, pardon and power. If grace were only pardon, our moral lives would never grow and we would go round and round a squirrel cage of I'm sorry, I forgive you, I'm sorry, I forgive you. If grace were only power, we would jerk back and forth from self-righteousness to despair; for while we can become better, we can never be perfect. Every day we need grace's pardon and power.

In his story, "The Happy Hypocrite," Max Beerbohm told of a debauched and unvirtuous man named Lord George Hell who fell in love with an innocent and saintly young woman. In order to woo and win her he covered his bloated features with the mask of a saint. The trick worked and the two were married. Years later a wicked lady from Lord George Hell's past showed up and sought to expose him for the scoundrel and fake she knew him to be. Confronting him in front of his wife, she dared him to take off his mask. Sadly he took it off—and to their great amazement discovered that beneath the mask of a saint was now the face of the saint he had become in wearing it.[7]

This is our hope—against all odds and all doubts—that as we follow Christ and "put him on," to borrow the language of the New Testament, He changes us who wear Him into His likeness. The apostle Paul said that as we behold His face we "are being changed into his likeness from one degree of glory to another" (2 Cor. 3:18).

Dr. Jekyll sought to be two people so that his good side could be good without the pull of evil and his evil side could be evil without the pang of guilt. His path was impossible. It is possible, however, to gain moral strength through grace—the grace of Jesus Christ which comes as pardon and power to those who invite Him into their lives and "put him on."

The moral tradition of the Judeo-Christian world offers invaluable resources to us as we seek to strengthen our moral character. One guidance of this tradition is the delineation of the *seven deadly sins;* another is the delineation of the *seven lively virtues.* These sets of sins and virtues will be our guide throughout this book toward the strengthening of our moral self.

Karl Menninger, a noted psychiatrist, wrote a book called *Whatever Became of Sin?*[8] It called for a renewal in our thought concerning the reality of sin. Alasdair MacIntyre, a prominent philosopher, wrote another recent book called *After Virtue*[9] which called for a renewed seriousness concerning the notion of virtue. Sin and virtue may be out of fashion, but they are not out of date. They may be out of our daily lexicons, but they are not out of our lives. Life can be better lived if we learn to control sin and if virtue trains us in the habit of goodness.

## The Sins

The church chose seven sins as particularly deadly: *Pride, Sloth, Envy, Anger, Greed, Gluttony, Lust.* Of course, these seven are not all of them. As Pogo said, "We have faults we have hardly used yet." Most of the ones we know, however, stem from these seven.

To consider the seven deadly sins is to take personal inventory. This enterprise also opens us up to God's grace, for these sins, and all sin, are obstacles to grace. Picture God's grace as the free flowing stream of love and power which God offers as a gift to flow through all His daughters and sons. Sin blocks the flow of grace. To consider the seven deadly sins is to become morally serious. As you do, the obstacles to grace will be toppled and you will experience grace's pardon and power.

## The Virtues

Just as important as the classification of the seven deadly sins is the classification of the virtues. The seven lively virtues I call them. Here are the seven virtues which the church picked out as the cream of the crop: *Wisdom, Courage, Justice, Temperance, Faith, Hope, Love.* The first four virtues—wisdom, courage, justice, and temperance—were adopted from the classical culture of Greece and Rome, baptized and given deeper meaning by the church. These four are often called the cardinal virtues, but we could call them civic virtues for they are essential virtues upon which the survival of our civilization depends.

The last three are taken from the Bible and are commonly called the theological virtues—faith, hope, and love. These virtues are gifts the Judeo-Christian community offers the world.

The virtues may not be as much fun as the sins. Virtue is never as entertaining to talk about as vice. The word *virtue* smacks of priggishness—a moral life based more on cowardice than on goodness, more manners than morals. We fear that virtues only make us what Mark Twain described as "a good man in the worst sense of the word."

In its original usage in the ancient Greek language, however, the word *virtue* (*arete*) meant *power*. Virtue is the active power of goodness, the power which helps you be happy, responsible, and free.

The seven deadly sins I call "obstacles to grace" because they block the gracious activity of God in our lives. I call the seven lively virtues "evidence of grace" because they manifest God's power of goodness within us. The first four, or classical virtues, are evidence of the grace of God present in all creation. All humanity may participate in these virtues apart from any religious faith. We, therefore, could call them evidence of natural grace. The last three virtues—faith, hope, and love—are a different story. These theological virtues are given by special grace of relationship to God through His covenant with Israel and in Jesus Christ. While all persons might have some measure of faith, hope, and love, these are given special force and shape within the Judeo-Christian heritage. Both sets of virtues are remarkable evidence of grace and are necessary to the flourishing of God's creatures and creation.

It is important to let our hearts and minds dwell on the power of goodness called virtue. There is too much of the tawdry and evil to dwell upon in our world. The apostle Paul took the list of virtues in his day, baptized them into the biblical world of meaning, and said: "Finally, brethren [and sisters], whatever is honorable, whatever is just, whatever is pure, whatever is lovely, whatever is gracious, if there is any excellence [*arete, virtue*], if there is anything worthy of praise, think about these things"

(Phil. 4:8). This book invites you to dwell on what is morally excellent.

* * * *

So here they are: The seven deadly sins and the seven lively virtues. Some smart aleck is bound to say, "They would better be called the seven lively sins and the seven deadly virtues." I have to admit, in our world the sins are colorful and lively characters while the virtues often come off as pale and stiff facsimiles of life. Nevertheless, the sins, however colorful and lively, eventually work their death in us; while the virtues, if they are God's power of goodness, bring us life.

Hopefully this book will bear out these truths while helping you escape the Jekyll and Hyde Syndrome. Because our lives are lived in the clash of two realms, one governed by the mystery of evil, the other by the mystery of goodness, a guided tour through the land of sins and virtues will help you live in the power of the former and escape the power of the latter. Your survival and the survival of our world depends upon our taking seriously the danger of sin and the importance of virtue.

### Notes

1.   Robert Louis Stevenson, *Dr. Jekyll and Mr. Hyde* (New York: Arco Publishing Company, 1964), p.78

2.   Ibid., pp. 78-79.

3.   John Updike, *Marry Me* (Greenwich, Conn.: Fawcett Books, 1971), p. 56.

4.   Willard Gaylin, *Feelings* (New York: Ballantine Books, 1978), p. 5.

5.   Quoted by C. S. Lewis, *The Screwtape Letters* (New York: The Macmillen Company, 1960), p. 7.

6.   Reinhold Niebuhr, *The Nature and Destiny of Man* (New York: Charles Scribner's Sons, 1964), pp. 98-119.

7.   Described by Frederick Buechner, *Telling the Truth* (New York: Harper & Row, 1977), p. 80

8.   Karl Menninger, *Whatever Became of Sin?* (New York: Hawthorn Books, Inc., 1973).

9.   Alasdair MacIntyre, *After Virtue* (Notre Dame, Ind.: University of Notre Dame Press, 1984).

# 1
# Whatever Became of Sin?

In our contemporary American society *"sin"* has become a buffoon's word. Society makes fun of the word, usually at the preacher's expense. "What did the preacher preach on today?" "Sin," was the reply. "Well, was he for it or against it?" Chuckle. A cartoon depicted a prophet figure decked out in sackcloth and ashes carrying a sign which read: "Resist Temptation." A rather seedy-looking character walked up, looked at the sign, and said: "Personally, I'm not interested in resisting temptation; I'm trying to *find* some."

Perhaps our laughter is a nervous laughter. We know deep down that sin is more a problem than we wish to admit. The Greeks thought that the root of all evil was *ignorance*. The Judeo-Christian heritage is more profound. It says that the root of all evil is not ignorance, but *sin*. Ph.Ds built the Nazi death camps. Suicide rates are highest in the most learned circles of our society. More than ignorance is at the root of our problems today. The problem is sin.

*Sin* is the word that stands for the wide range of actions and attitudes which separate us from or turn us against God, our own true self, and neighbor. Sin also disrupts the delicate ecological balance of nature and society.

It was a psychiatrist, Karl Menninger, who was brave to raise the question, *Whatever Became of Sin?*[1] He made the point that the word *sin* has virtually disappeared from public discourse.

No President of the United States, for example, used the word in public address between 1953 and 1973. Along with the word's disappearance has come the disappearance of a sense of moral responsibility, which Menninger also confronts.

In the nineteenth century, most sins were given a new name: crimes. Policemen and courtrooms took over from the clergy and churches. At the turn of the twentieth century there came another change with the advent of psychoanalysis and other psychiatric breakthroughs: sins changed from crimes to sicknesses. Psychiatrists and hospitals replaced policemen and courtrooms. In Aldous Huxley's *Brave New World* an announcement is made that someone had committed a crime which elicited the "compassionate" response, "I did not know he was ill."[2]

We presently live in that "new world." Today sins are thought of as sickness or symptoms of illness. Freud's psychic determinism has been misused to excuse immoral and antisocial behavior. No longer do we have bad children, only bad parents; no longer do we have criminals, only bad environmental conditions. Insanity has become a frequent defense for murder with psychiatrists becoming chief expert witnesses for the defense. Willard Gaylin, M.D., psychiatrist, practicing psychoanalyst, philosopher, and author argues that the insanity defense which in his words "has served the noblest spirit in modern civilization" has been "degraded to the point of a professional embarrassment."[3] In his brilliant and disturbing study, *The Killing of Bonnie Garland,* Gaylin chronicles the misuse of psychiatric testimony during the trial of Richard Herrin who killed his Yale girl friend while she slept. Gaylin not only questioned his peer group, the psychiatrists, in their participation, but also the legal profession and the Christian community which immediately came to the murderer's aid. All participated in a process that undermined the notion of moral responsibility, community morality, and social justice. This case is a microcosm of the confusion at large in our society.[4] Our superficial and/or inappropriate application of psychoanalytic thought has led us down the road to excusing the most abhorrent behavior. A poem pokes fun at this spirit of the times:

> At three I had a feeling of
>     Ambivalence toward my brothers,
> And so it follows naturally
>     I poisoned all my lovers.
> But now I'm happy; I have learned
>     The lesson this has taught
> That everything I do that's wrong
>     Is someone else's fault.

Neither Menninger, Gaylin, nor I would wish to suggest it would be better to leap-frog back and live as if no advancements had been made the past 200 years. It has proven to be a humane discovery that some behaviors we thought were sins or crimes are sicknesses. However, we must not misuse these medical and scientific insights to obscure the basic notion of moral responsibility. We are responsible for those attitudes and actions which separate us from (or turn us against) God, our own true self, and neighbor.

There are signs that our society is recovering some recognition of the reality of sin. Ethics courses at professional graduate schools are proliferating. New questions are being asked about value-free education and the glamour of secularity. Moral education is a popular new discipline. The resurgence of the "religious right" and political conservatism has been fueled by the sense that something has gone wrong in America and that at the core of the gone-wrongness is moral lassitude. Books like Henry Fairlie's *The Seven Deadly Sins Today* have caused us to take a fresh look at sin. Even *Esquire* magazine had a recent (July 1986) cover article called "A Modern Guide to the Seven Deadly Sins." Seven famous authors wrote essays on the sins. Some of the essays were more a guide to the committing of the sins than to avoiding them, making virtues of the sins or trivializing them. Three of the authors, however, actually wrote as if their assigned sins were really deadly: Roy Blount, Jr. on avarice, William F. Buckley on envy, and Garrison Keillor on lust (Keillor is in my estimation America's most persuasive moralist—a designation which would ruin his reputation).

This book is a call to the recovery of a sense of moral responsibility. With apologies to Shakespeare, a sin by any other name is still a sin. We are responsible and moral failure can reap terrible harvests.

A life of well-being and well-doing is possible for everyone. The truly good life is a life happy, responsible, and free. Such a life is a possibility for anyone who would be morally serious and for anyone who takes seriously the reality, strength, and reach of sin.

## The Bible and Sin

The Bible is the truest and most realistic book in the world regarding human nature. The first thing it says about sin is that sin is **real.** The rebellion of Adam and Eve, Cain's murder of Abel, the injustice of kings, the barbarity of nation-states, the plundering of God's earth—all of these are biblical depictions of the reality of sin's devastation.

The Bible also insists that sin is **personal,** at least in its origins. Sin begins in the inner recesses of the human heart. We cannot escape responsibility by saying, "The devil made me do it," nor may we say, "My mother made me do it," or "These drugs made me do it." Jesus would not let us "pass the buck":

> Hear me, all of you, and understand: there is nothing outside a man which by going into him can defile him; but the things which come out of a man are what defile him. . . . from within, out of the heart of man, come evil thoughts, fornication [*porneia*] theft, murder, adultery, coveting, wickedness, deceit, licentiousness, envy, slander, pride, foolishness (Mark 7:14-15, 21-22).

Jesus is not suggesting that there is no presence of sin (or evil) outside of us which can exert its influence. He is, rather, suggesting that the origin of sin is always inner, and that whatever influence outer powers may have, it is our choice whether to let these influences sway us.

The Bible goes on then to say that sin is **strong.** Here is where the language of "demon possession" becomes pertinent. In the New Testament we witness Jesus freeing people from the power of demons or unclean spirits. Some of these episodes suggest that what the person suffered was what we would today call psychiatric (for example, schizophrenia) or neurological (for example, epilepsy) disorders. However, many of these people suffered a moral sickness. We are told that Jesus freed Mary Magdalene from seven demons (Luke 8:2). In the vernacular of the concrete, ethically minded Jewish culture, this language, "seven demons," probably represented something akin to our seven deadly sins. It was a way of saying that her life was completely given over to an immoral existence, like being consumed by all seven deadly sins at once.

The image of demonic possession suggests the outer limits of what sin can do to us. Sin is more than an action or attitude; it may also be a power which can control us. We give in to the ways of sin until we no longer have control of it; it has control over us. Witness the demise of good Dr. Jekyll who in trying to dally with sin and be good one day and bad the next was overtaken by the evil side, Mr. Hyde.

The Bible goes on to say that sin is **social.** Sin which begins in the human heart may become embedded in social customs, institutions, and structures. The New Testament calls the extrapersonal, or suprapersonal, manifestations of sin "principalities and powers." Personal sin thereby turns into historical, social, and political sin. What began "inside of us" is now outside of us and acts back on us. Sociologists Peter Berger and Thomas Luckmann describe the process this way:

> Society is a human product.
> Society is an objective reality.
> Man is a social product.[5]

Unjust social structures, ideologies, racism and sexism, The Third Reich, policies which allow environmental destruction are all examples of sins that have reached social and institutional dimension. Sin present in these "principalities and powers" is enormously powerful, acts back upon us, shaping our personal and social existence.

Finally the Bible tells us that sin is *serious.* While this book will poke fun at the sins and at our inclination to sin, I would not intimate that sin is not serious. In a startlingly stern passage Jesus warned:

> Whoever causes one of these little ones who believe in me to sin, it would be better for him if a great millstone were hung around his neck and he were thrown into the sea. And if your hand causes you to sin cut it off; it is better for you to enter life maimed than with two hands to go to hell (Mark 9:42-43).

Why do we consider our physical health so much more important than our moral health? Jesus argues that if we had gangrene in the foot we would not hesitate to amputate it in order to save the leg or our life. We need to be just as serious about our moral health as our physical health. Sin is that serious, yet many of us play around with sin like a game of Russian roulette.

## Categories of Sin

There are any number of ways we could catagorize the sins. The Old Testament had three words for sin: (1) *Transgression* which means willful rebellion against God; (2) *Sin* or "missing the mark" which means failure to achieve the goal; and (3) *Iniquity* which means to overstep the law.

Perhaps the most poignant meaning of sin in the Bible is sin as *infidelity.* Sin is more than a breaking of rules, it is the breaking of relationships. The sinful person is pictured as the son who willfully rebels against his father or as an unfaithful spouse. "Israel has gone whoring after false gods" was the prophet Hosea's warning and the analogy used was a woman who went after other lovers.

Sin is unfaithfulness. It involves breaking the relationship of covenant-love with God. All sin, therefore, is *relational* in character. It disrupts the most basic of all relationships: your relationship with God, with your own true self, and with neighbor. It makes you a stranger to God, to others, and even to yourself. The pathos of the sinful life is that it does far more than break rules. It breaks hearts: God's heart, the hearts of those you love, and, finally, your own heart.

Dorothy Sayers divides the sins into two groups—hot and cold.[6] The coldhearted sins are pride, envy, and greed. The warmhearted sins are sloth, gluttony, and lust. Anger can be either the hot burst of temper or the cold brooding sin of bitterness.

I have another way of classifying the sins: crazy, mean, and stupid. *Stupid sins* are things you do that hurt yourself and others out of ignorance. You do something and say afterward, "Boy, was that dumb!" Being smart about what is good for you is important. Some things are simply *dumb*—from alcohol and drug abuse to laziness and procrastination. We can all use help in learning rules for sensible and successful living so that we avoid the stupid sins.

*Crazy sins* are things you do that you know will cause damage, but you do them anyway. They are what psychiatrists call "reality-disregarding." You do things you know are self-destructive. You, for example, lie, knowing you can be caught. Or, you get involved in an extramarital affair knowing that there is only bad news ahead. Alice Munro, in *The Moons of Jupiter*, said that there are points in time when, in her words, "What you have to decide, really, is whether to be crazy or not."[7] She goes on: "There is a limit to the amount of misery and disarray you will put up with, for love, just as there is a limit to the amount of mess you can stand around a house." Time comes when we say, "Enough craziness!"

*Mean sins* are just that: mean. They are what we used to call being ornery. We willfully inflict pain on others: slander's sharp tongue, greed's cold heart, envy's evil eye, acts of personal cruelty.

The Bible lists hundreds of sins, from the Ten Commandments to Jesus' list of thirteen. There are hot sins and cold ones, crazy, mean, and stupid ones, sins that break rules and sins that break hearts, but perhaps the best-known classification of sin are the seven we now investigate. This classification is a helpful tool in taking moral inventory. The seven deadly sins were first officially classified as such by Gregory the Great around AD 600, but they probably were classified informally long before that. They have surely withstood the test of time. Let us now take a look at them—that we may more truthfully see ourselves.

### Notes

1. Karl Menninger, *Whatever Became of Sin?* (New York: Hawthorn Books, Inc., 1973).

2. Willard Gaylin, *The Killing of Bonnie Garland* (New York: Penguin Books, 1983), p. 342.

3. Ibid., p. 15.

4. Ibid. See also Robert Cole's reviews in *The New Yorker* (July 26, 1982), pp. 39-95. Gaylin remarks about the extraordinary lack of revulsion in those who had contact with the killer. For another study in the phenomenon of evil and of the appropriate response of revulsion to evil see Mr. Scott Peck, *People of the Lie: The Hope for Healing Human Evil* (New York: Simon and Schuster, 1983).

5. Peter Berger and Thomas Luckmann, *The Social Construction of Reality* (New York: Doubleday and Company, 1966), p. 58.

6. Dorothy L. Sayers, "The Other Six Deadly Sins," in her *Creed and Chaos* (New York: Harcourt, Brace and Company, 1949).

7. Alice Munro, *The Moons of Jupiter* (New York: Viking Penguin, Inc., 1984), p. 127.

PRIDE *is camel-nosed.*

PRIDE GOES BEFORE destruction AND A HAUGHTY SPIRIT BEFORE a fall.

# 2
# Pride

The first sin to consider is *pride*. It is always first on the list. If the seven sins are pictured as limbs of a tree, often pride is pictured as the trunk of the tree. That may be overstating the case. Pride may not be the root of all the others; however, it could hardly be denied that pride makes the other six deadly sins deadlier.

Pride makes envy greener and anger meaner. It makes our greed greedier and gluttony "eatier." Sloth becomes lazier and lust lustier. Pride infects all vices and all virtues. Its reach is long and its roots are deep. And as one has said: "It comes early and stays late."

## I

What is pride? Dictionaries often define it as "inordinate self-esteem." The Old Testament has six Hebrew words which translate as pride. They have the sense of "to lift up" or "to be on high."

Each of the sins has its own face. The association between an animal and a sin is frequently made. One has said that pride is "camel-nosed."[1] Have you ever seen a humble-looking camel? The nose is high and lifted up. "Stuck-up" is another expression used. High-blown, puffed-up. Or a newer expression: "He's eat up with himself."

Pride is also seen as being "inordinately pleased with one

self." The chest is swollen; a walk turns into a strut. Another animal is invoked: "Proud as a peacock."

But isn't pride a *good* thing too, you ask? Shouldn't we take pride in ourselves? If the sin of pride is inordinate self-esteem, isn't there an ordinate, a proper amount of self-esteem, self-respect, or self-worth?

These questions are given a quick and facile yes by most people today. Erich Fromm suggests that you must love yourself before you can love another. Aristotle identified pride not as the root of all sin but as the crown of all virtue *if* pride achieves the golden mean between two extremes—extreme vanity or extreme humiliation. Even Jesus implies the need of self-love in the commandment to love the neighbor as yourself (Mark 12:29-31). And Paul's warning was not to think more highly of yourself than you ought to think (Rom. 12:3).

Yes, I think that most people would agree—we need a kind of pride that avoids thinking too highly or too lowly of oneself. One extreme is the sin of pride; the other—thinking too lowly—is sloth, as we shall see in the next chapter. We want to avoid the arrogance of a Mr. Cool or the poor-mouthed groveling of Mr. Milquetoast.

## II

If some pride is constructive, what is this deep dark sin called pride? The Bible traces pride all the way back to the Garden of Eden.

God created us male and female and gave us dominion over His world. We were given the charge to name and arrange His world; that is, God made us His partners in finishing creation. But when God placed some restrictions on freedom and dominion—"Do not eat of this tree!"—Adam and Eve rebelled. Davie Napier captures their rebellion in his book *Come Sweet Death.* Adam addresses God:

> You speak a pious, childish doggerel
> that sings like "Mary Had a Little Lamb"

Freely eat of every tree
every tree every tree
freely eat of every tree
    nothing I deny
but the tree of good and evil
good and evil good and evil
but the tree of good and evil
    eat of it and die.

Behold, God's wondrous gift is given—with strings.
All glory be to thee, uncertain Giver,
who wants to have His gift and give it too.
I know about your . . . restricted tree:
it symbolizes you and your dominion.
To spare its fruit is to acknowledge you.

Now hear this, Lord: the Giver with the gift
is strictly for the birds and fish and beasts.
I am a Man, made in the godly image,
made to receive and rule the gift of God.
God is for giving, Give, then, and get out.[2]

Adam and Eve cut God off so God banished them from the Garden. History then becomes the story of the uses and misuses of our dominion because of the sin of pride. And the Bible becomes a constant warning against our pride.

The Tower of Babel warns those who wish to build a tower to heaven and become as God. The prophets perceived the pride of nations. Ezekiel tells a story about a great cedar grown tall, strong, and beautiful at the bank of a river. But the tree forgets that its nourishment comes from the river. Because the tree refuses to acknowledge the source of its power, God destroys it (Ezek. 31:1-14).

Solomon, who did not always practice what he preached, said in Proverbs 16:18, "Pride goeth before destruction, and a haughty spirit before a fall" (KJV).

The apostle Paul saw pride at the root of all sin: Sin is refusing to honor God or to give thanks to God. We exchange, Paul teaches, the glory of the immortal God for the images of mortal man (Rom. 1:18-32). We trade in the Bible for a mirror, worshiping not the Creator but our own creatureliness.

So the quip is correct: The problem with the self-made man is that he worships his creator.

## III

Pride, then, at base is an *idolatry of the self.* As the serpent tempted Adam and Eve, he tempts us: We want to be as gods. And if you look more closely you see that the root of the desire is in anxiety. The serpent suggests that God really does not have our best interests at heart. We become fearful, anxious. Our mistrust is bred until we strike out on our own. Reinhold Niebuhr was right: Anxiety is the root of pride. We set up human idols of self to take God's place and secure ourselves against pain and death.[3]

Historically, the church has identified pride's three main idols: pride of power, pride of knowledge, and pride of goodness. Here we observe the insidious character of pride. As Dorothy Sayers comments: "The devilish strategy of Pride is that it attacks us not on our weak points, but on our strong."[4]

The pride of power seizes power, forgetting that all power comes from God (Rom. 13:1-2), making it an idol. We turn dominion over the earth into a plundering of the earth. Our streams are poisoned and the air polluted. In the words of Joni Mitchell, we have "paved paradise and put up a parking lot." We've trusted in the right of might instead of the might of right. In our bravado we strut over the face of God's earth while filling our basements with nuclear bombs. The pride of power. As the Promethean One, we steal fire from the gods and call it ours.

Then there is the pride of knowledge. We make an idol out of our learning. We look down our noses at the vulgar ignorance of the crowd. We trust in our theories. We want to know everything and like Dr. Faust we sell our souls for ultimate knowledge. As the Faustian One, we eat of the tree of knowledge and call ourselves God.

There is also the pride of goodness. It is the special sin of

Pharisees, the religious self-righteous ones of all ages. Like the
Pharisee in Jesus' story, we pray:

*I thank you Lord that I am not like other folks. I am a*
*born-again Christian. . . . I keep my body pure. . . . I pray every*
*day whether I need to or not. . . . I vote against liquor by the*
*drink. . . . I support Bread For the World. . . . I thank God I am*
*not like other folks. Amen.*

Saint Bernard said of the proud monk: "He is inclined to fast
more, pray longer, sleep less, look sicker than his fellows, prov-
ing that he is a *singular* holy man."[5] The pride of goodness. As
the Pharisaical One we trust in our goodness.

## IV

These are the three big branches of pride: power, knowledge,
and goodness. But there are many little branches sprouting out
from these.

The spirit of *vanity.* The vain person walks down the street
as if every person is looking at him or her. Carly Simon had a
song about a vain boyfriend; the main line was: "You're so vain,
you probably think this song is about you."

The Bible and many sermons since have warned about *osten-*
*tation*—the display of lavish clothing and jewelry. One brave
preacher preached on that topic and after the service was ac-
costed by an extravagantly attired woman. "Are my clothes all
right?" she asked. "Better so," he answered. "If you have the
spirit of vanity, better to hang out the sign, so people may be
warned."

Then there is the pride of rebelliousness against all authority. Do you chafe under authority figures? **Contumacy,** the
Parson called this form of Pride in his sermon on the Seven
Deadly Sins in Chaucer's *The Canterbury Tales.*[6] It is a favorite
form of pride today. We see ourselves above all forms of authority.

There is **conceit** and **scorn.** And there are more branches
still. Pride pokes out its head when we must win arguments;
when we force others to admit their mistakes, sometimes over

and over;[7] when we are impatient with others; when we say "If I had the time, I'd do it myself"; when we are sure who is right and who is wrong in every conflict.

Pride is also seen, says the Parson in *The Canterbury Tales*, in **chattering:** "When men speak too much before folk, clattering like a mill and taking no care of what they say."[8]

Pride is at work in *false humility.* "Oh shucks, it was nothing" often drips with pride. As Pascal noted, "Few speak of humility humbly."

## V

There are many branches to pride. To examine yourself is to see far more pride than you suspect. As Augustine said, pride is both cold and blind.[9] Pride is deadly because it blinds us to its own presence. If you do not think you have pride, watch out!

Pride is also cold. Color it blue. It moves us in the words of William May into "the shadow of solitude."[10] It's lonely at the top. We pride ourselves in our uniqueness. This may even take the form of priding ourselves in the uniqueness of our suffering or hardship. In all cases it moves us toward aloneness. That is why one of the main words for pride in church literature is *singularity.* Quite unique, we are quite alone.

## VI

These are some of the shapes and shades of pride. Pride is an obstacle to grace because it implies no need of God. Pride is a stronghold. But thanks be to God: Sin is strong, but grace is stronger!

Grace comes in the twin form of pardon and power. By grace we are healed and delivered. To it's great surprise, pride discovers that this grace comes in the form of a cross, that its salvation comes in a crucified Messiah. No strength of your own can help you receive this grace. Your strengths, to the contrary, keep you from the foot of the cross, because the ground at the foot of the cross is always level. No one is higher than another.

One thing and one thing only brings you there—that is the sense of need.

Dante pictured sinners being cleansed of their sins in purgatory. The first terrace up the purgatorial mountain was where Dante's pilgrims were being cleansed of pride. We see them walking over a marble pavement covered with sculptured figures which preach silent sermons on true humility.[11]

Imagine walking along that path. There is Moses who "wist not his face shone." There is the publican who cried, "Have mercy on me a sinner." There is Mary kneeling in submission to God's awesome will. And there is Jesus, "Who though he was in the form of God did not count equality with God a thing to be grasped, but emptied himself, taking the form of a servant, being born in the likeness of men. And being found in human form he humbled himself and became obedient unto death, even death on a cross" (Phil. 2:6-8).

Before such a horrid cross, can we be proud? We cannot receive its grace and still be proud. It is the final most deadly character of pride that it keeps us from the very place where we can find healing: the cross.

### Notes

1.  Angus Wilson quoted in Henry Fairlie, *The Seven Deadly Sins Today* (Washington, D. C.: New Republic Books, 1978), p. 41. (Hereafter designated as Fairlie.)

2.  Davie B. Napier, *Come Sweet Death* (Philadelphia: United Church Press, 1967), pp. 19-20.

3.  Reinhold Niebuhr, *The Nature and Destiny of Man* (New York: Charles Schribner's Sons, 1964) Vol. I, pp. 181 ff.

4.  Dorothy L. Sayers, "The Other Six Deadly Sins," *Creed or Chaos* (New York: Harcourt, Brace and Company, 1949), p. 83. (Hereafter designated as Sayers.)

5.  Saint Bernard, *The Steps of Humility* (London: H. R. Mowbray and Co. Ltd., 1957), p. 69. (Italics mine)

6.  Chaucer, Geoffrey, *The Canterbury Tales* in Great Books of the Western World (Chicago: Encyclopaedia Britannica, Inc., 1952), p. 511. (Hereafter designated as Chaucer.)

7.  See Wayne Oates, "Pastoral Examples and Procedures in Diagnosis and Treatment of the Seven Deadly Sins," an unpublished essay, p. 1.

8. Chaucer, p. 511.

9. Quoted in William F. May, *A Catalogue of Sins* (New York: Holt; Rinehard and Winston, 1967), p. 185. (Hereafter designated as May.)

10. May, pp. 175 ff.

11. Dante Alighieri, *The Divine Comedy*, "Purgatory" in Great Books of the Western World (Chicago: Encyclopaedia Britannica, Inc., 1952), pp. 56 ff. (Hereafter designated as Dante.)

IN THE WORLD IT CALLS ITSELF
TOLERANCE,
BUT IN HELL IT IS CALLED
DESPAIR...SLOTH...ACCOMPLICE
TO THE OTHER SINS AND THEIR WORST
PUNISHMENT

IT is the sin which believes in
NOTHING
CARES FOR NOTHING
SEEKS TO KNOW NOTHING
INTERFERES WITH NOTHING
ENJOYS NOTHING
LOVES NOTHING
HATES NOTHING
FINDS PURPOSE IN NOTHING
LIVES FOR NOTHING
and only remains alive because
there is NOTHING it would
die for.

# 3
# Sloth

Sloth is normally associated with laziness. *Webster's* defines it as the "disinclination to action and labor." An animal is easy to come up with: A sloth, that South American animal normally seen hanging upside down from branches. Or picture the hibernating bear. As William May puts it: "The great brown bear drowses in all of us, the spirit of hibernation, so profound, so soothing."[1]

From infancy we have been warned against laziness. It was a sin not just against God (and the Puritan work ethic), but against the American way of life. So we learned the stories of "The Little Red Hen" and of the industrious ant and the lazy grasshopper (the origin of which is Prov. 6:6-11).

One could argue that our culture thereby has produced a legion of "workaholics," to use Wayne Oates's word,[2] and that we need a bit of sloth. The Italians have a phrase *dulce far niente* which translates *the sweet doing nothing*. We all need some time every week when we can enjoy the sweet doing of nothing.

However, we would trivialize the sin of sloth if we kept it within these kinds of categories. For sloth is far deeper than laziness. It may be one of the most devastating of the seven deadly sins today.

# I

The word used for the sin of sloth in the Greek is *akedia,* or in the Latin *accidia.* The literal meaning is *no caring*—close to our word *apathy.* Color it drab and think of despondency, discouragement, dejection, despair. In prescientific times its usage described depression and referred to that melancholy spirit to which the psalmist perhaps spoke when he talked of the "destruction that wastes at noonday" (Ps. 91:6).

I believe at this point we must be very careful not to identify the sin of sloth with all kinds of depression. There are physiological forms of depression that are not the result or symptom of sin. Other depressions are caused by traumatic events inflicted on the person. It would be cruel to call depressive illness a sin.

Having clarified that, I acknowledge that a spiritual malaise called sloth or *akedia* exists which cannot be attributed to physiological imbalance or to traumatizing circumstances. That is the sin which we address.

# II

What are the roots of sloth? Let us go back to the Garden of Eden. God has created His beautiful and intricate universe, the earth and its creatures, and as the very crown of creation, God creates man and woman in His own image. He then gives them dominion over the earth. Their charge is to name and arrange God's creation, thereby becoming God's partners in the finishing of creation.

Now imagine a slightly different scenario than the one you are used to. In another part of the Garden of Eden live George and Martha, younger brother and sister of Adam and Eve.

One day when George and Martha were busy at their chores the serpent slithered up to George (sensing him to be the more vulnerable of the two) and asked: "How would you like to eat of the tree of knowledge of good and evil?" George replied, "Are you kidding! We have enough to do as it is—naming and arranging, tilling and tending. One thing I don't need is something more to learn and to do."

The serpent drew back, pondered the situation for a moment, and then said: "You are absolutely right, George. You really have too much to do. It is quite unreasonable for God to expect that much. What about overtime? No overtime! Don't you ever wonder whether you can do it all? Listen, I've got a better idea. Why don't you come with me and leave this garden. Hey, you deserve a break today! You need to be more laid back. Go with the flow, George. Que sera, sera. You get Martha and we'll all go get mellow."

So George went to Martha; they talked it over. Giving up their calling to be children of God, they left the garden and became children of sloth.

### III

Granted, that isn't the version you've heard, but it gets reenacted every day. It was Harvey Cox and his book *On Not Leaving It to the Snake* who first suggested to me that the fall might have to do with sloth as well as pride.[3] Sloth is casting aside your call to be a son or daughter made in God's image and instead deciding to live as a lower animal.

Pride and sloth represent two opposite but deadly sins. Pride is the attempt to be more than human; sloth is the attempt to be less than human. Pride seeks God's throne; sloth runs from the Garden. Pride takes on God's role; sloth escapes human responsibility.

Pride and sloth are the two major sins committed in the Garden of God. Pride takes the dominion God has given us and turns it into destruction, a plundering of the earth for our own purposes. God sang a sad love song through Isaiah: I gave you my vineyard, built a fence, cleared it for planting. But what have you done? I looked for sweet grapes and found sour ones. I looked for justice and heard only a cry of distress (see Isa. 5:1-7). Pride is the story of dominion turned sour.

The opposite sin is sloth. Sloth refuses to exercise dominion given. It flees responsibility. Proverbs tells a story of sloth in the vineyard: "I passed by the field of a [slothful man], . . . and lo, it was all overgrown with thorns; the ground was covered with nettles and its stone wall was broken down" (Prov. 24:30-31).

We are beginning to get at the root. Pride thinks too highly of itself. Sloth thinks too lowly. Pride presumes to be more than human. Sloth is content to be less than human. Pride usurps the place of God; sloth abdicates the role of human kind.

## IV

We see sloth all about us today. If the former generation gloried in its hard work, this generation has raised sloth to be a virtue. Industry, excellence, and goodness are mocked. Scornful of competition, we enshrine mediocrity.

As there is pride in power, knowledge, and goodness, there is also sloth in each. If there is a pride of power, sloth is the refusal to exercise power. We refuse to develop the powers and talents God has given us. We cover up the image of God. The tragedy is that power like nature abhors a vacuum, hence, if good persons do not exercise power judiciously, evil persons are waiting in line to exercise it ruthlessly. In the famous words attributed to Edmund Burke, "The only thing necessary for the triumph of evil is for good men to do nothing."

If there is pride in knowledge, there is also intellectual sloth. American life is filled with sloth in the form of antiintellectualism. We seek shortcuts to truth. We crave easy answers politically and religiously. All truth is reduced to slogans. What we call an intellectual debate is a collision of bumper stickers. Make Love, Not War! America: Love It or Leave It. We grasp at easy truths. I have some advice: Any truth that can be put on a bumper sticker is not worth putting on a bumper sticker. Learning goes down in our schools, but grades go up. The vocabulary in use in America has dropped dramatically the past fifty years.

If there can be pride in goodness, there is also spiritual sloth.

We think we can become instant saints. One recent book's title is *EST: 60 Hours that Transform Your Life.* Book stores are filled with promises to transform you and offer instant salvation. One has called these "Do-It-Yourself-God Kits." That may appear to be a form of pride. Just as likely it is sloth—the desire for shortcuts to goodness. The next religious best-seller will be *10 Easy Steps to the Devout and Holy Life.*

Sloth is all about us in our "laid-back," "Go with the Flow" culture. There is what one has called "The Misty-eyed Gestalt Prayer" of Fritz Perls that you have seen on a thousand posters: "You are you and I am I, and if by chance we find each other, it's beautiful."[4] (Can you imagine Jesus saying anything like that?) There is sloth in what Chaucer's Parson calls negligence: It "cares not, when it must do a thing, whether it be done well or badly."[5] Sloth has many forms.

# V

If pride is the idolatry of the self, sloth is the giving up of the self, the loss of selfhood. Reinhold Niebuhr enumerated the two major sins as pride and sensuality and what he described as sensuality is a dimension of what I call here sloth—the loss of the self in some other force or impulse.[6]

You may begin now to see why sloth is so deadly. Dorothy Sayers has described it in its most chilling dimension:

> In the world it calls itself Tolerance, but in hell it is called Despair. It is the accomplice of the other sins and their worst punishment. It is the sin which believes in nothing, cares for nothing, seeks to know nothing, interferes with nothing, enjoys nothing, loves nothing, hates nothing, finds purpose in nothing, lives for nothing, and only remains alive because there is nothing it would die for.[7]

Sloth is the deadening reality of boredom; it is the state of weariness and dissatisfaction with life the French call *ennui.* It is the feeling that "It doesn't matter."

Sloth is a form of grief, but different at a crucial point. In true grief one is sad at the loss of a loved one. In sloth one grieves in the presence of a loved one.[8] A man is bored by his son. A spouse finds that the feeling is gone. He says his spouse no longer stirs him. He takes no delight in the beloved. He failed to grasp one truth: Your spouse is not just bone of your bone and flesh of your flesh but is also "boredom of your boredom and lovelessness of your lovelessness."[9]

The slothful person is tempted to run from family, job, and church and go roaming around the country unattached and free.[10] Novels and movies have explored this kind of sloth: Updike's *Rabbit Run;* the movie *5 Easy Pieces.*

Sloth has lost its taste for life in the presence of life. So describes Proverbs 12:27: "The slothful man roasteth not that which he took in hunting" (KJV). Like James Joyce's hero in *A Portrait of the Artist as a Young Man:* "Nothing moved him or spoke to him from the real world. . . . He could respond to no earthly or human appeal, dumb and insensible to the call of summer and gladness and companionship."[11]

And this boredom with life extends to a boredom with God. You are untouched and unmoved in the presence of God. That is the sloth Thomas Aquinas called "sorrow in the Divine good,"[12] or what Augustine described as "the sadness of goodness."[13]

Sloth works its way through some of the other sins. Gluttony and lust may be the way of losing the self you no longer care for. "Why do you drink?" asked the young lady in William Saroyan's play, *The Time of Your Life.* Joe replied, "Why does anyone drink?" Then he explains:

> Every day has 24 hours . . . out of the 24 hours at least 23 1/2 are—my God, I don't know why—dull, dead, boring, empty, and murderous. Minutes on the clock, not time of living . . . but spent in waiting . . . and the more you wait, the less there is to wait for . . . That goes on for days and days and weeks and months and years and years and the first thing you know all the years are dead. All the minutes are dead. You yourself are dead.[14]

You begin to see why sloth is "an accomplice" of other sins. Slothful, we drown ourselves in impulses or in alcohol and drugs. "No-caring," we anesthetize ourselves with TV's monotonous gaggle. Bored with life, we go wherever the most exciting momentary diversion lies.

It becomes clearer why sloth is not only an accomplice of other sins but their worst punishment. A vicious cycle is set in motion. You think so lowly of yourself that you give yourself up to unworthy actions. These actions themselves produce a kind of despondency, a feeling of helplessness and hopelessness.

As T. S. Elliot prophesied, we become the hollow men, the stuffed men, and the world ends "Not with a bang but a whimper."[15]

## VI

A terrifying picture of sin is presented. Do you see why sloth is an obstacle to grace? Thinking too lowly of ourselves we doubt grace, refuse grace, and may even find ourselves bored in its presence.

Hear now the gospel. Sin is strong, but grace is stronger.

You are a child of God created by God as an act of love, an act of love He saw and called good. You were created in the image of God. The image is Christ; you bear it on your heart as the truest truth about you.

You are the crown of God's creation, the apple of God's eye. He has blessed you and called you to be His companion in the finishing of creation.

God sent His Son to reveal who you are and to give you the power to be who you are. "To all who received him, . . . he gave power to become children of God" (John 1:12).

You have the most exciting purpose in all the world as a citizen in the kingdom of God seeking to penetrate this world like salt and like light. You are the light of the world! You are God's work of art created in Christ Jesus for good works (Eph. 2:10). You are the body of Christ. Your hands are Christ's hands; your heart is His heart. You say you can't win the battle over sloth? God gives you the Holy Spirit poured into your hearts as Christ's own love, and with the Spirit you are given faith and hope, you are given courage, joy, and peace. The power to be a son or a daughter of God is yours.

Awake your souls from sloth. There is work to do for God. Not dreary work, but the glad work of love; not work doomed for failure, but labor in a kingdom whose victory is assured. In the words of folksinger Darrell Adams, "We are running the race that God has won."

Arise, Christians, run, work, and love; laugh and sing. Leap for joy, you belong to God.

## Notes

1. May, p. 191.
2. Wayne Oates, *Confessions of a Workaholic* (New York: World Publishing, 1971).
3. Harvey Cox, *On Not Leaving It to the Snake* (New York: The Macmillan Co., 1964).
4. Quoted in Fairlie, p. 117.
5. Chaucer, p. 528.
6. Reinhold Niebuhr, *The Nature and Destiny of Man,* p. 228 ff.
7. Sayers, p. 81.
8. May, p. 195.
9. Helmut Thieliche, *How the World Began* (Philadelphia: Muhlenburg Press, 1961), p. 99.
10. Wayne Oates, "Pastoral Examples . . .," p. 14.
11. Quoted in May, p. 196.
12. Thomas Aquinas, *Summa Theologica* II Great Books of the Western World, Vol. 20 (Chicago: Encyclopaedia Britannica, Inc., 1952), p. 563. (Hereafter designated Aquinas.)
13. Quoted in Chaucer, p. 526.
14. Quoted in Laner Webb, *Conquering the Seven Deadly Sins* (New York: Abingdon Press, 1955), p. 110.
15. T. S. Eliot, "The Hollow Men," *The Complete Poems and Plays* (New York: Harcourt, Brace and Co., 1952), pp. 56-59.

ENVY IS THE SIN OF AN EVIL EYE

Envy is
the sorrow at
another's success
and the joy
at another's
misfortune.

IS YOUR EYE EVIL BECAUSE I AM GOOD?

# 4
# Envy

Oscar Wilde told a story of a religious hermit so Christian and so holy that the evil spirits sent to tempt him ended up defeated and discouraged. They could not break him down. They tried passions of the body, doubts of the mind; they even tried to provoke pride in his goodness, but every temptation failed. Then Satan himself came to the evil spirits and said, "Your methods are crude. Permit me one moment." So, going to the holy hermit, Satan said: "Have you heard the good news?! Your brother has been made Bishop of Alexandria." That got him. "My brother, Bishop of Alexandria!" *Envy swept through him like a tidal wave.*

Envy has been called the ugliest and meanest of the seven deadly sins. In Chaucer's *The Canterbury Tales*, the Parson calls it "a foul sin." Surely it is. The other sins may be against one special virtue (for example, pride is against humility), but envy sneers its face "against all virtues and against all goodness."[1] And while the other sins have some early pay-off, some early delight, envy from the beginning is endless anguish and self-torment.

A color is easy to come up with. "Green with Envy." Even the color is the ugliest. It may look good on Kermit the Frog (though Kermit out of envy wishes to be another color), it is certainly dear to the Irish on Saint Patrick's Day, it looks good on your lawn and is a favorite to all preppies out there, but you

don't want to turn green. Green of complexion is associated
with sickness. And green is also used in another image of envy:
"The grass is always greener on the other side of the fence."
That is envy's fix.

Envy's face is the ugliest, uglier than pride's camel nose or
sloth's sad and vacant eyes or anger's flushed face and flared
nostrils. Envy has slit eyes—eyes narrowed and severe. The
New Testament Greek phrase for envy is literally to have an
"evil eye," to look upon with evil.

Envy is a sin of the eyes. A partner gets a promotion and the
eyes turn evil. A beautiful woman walks into a room, and while
the men gaze upon her with what may be another of the seven
deadly sins, a woman finds that her eyes turn evil with envy.

The Latin word for envy is *invidia*. It means to look mali-
ciously upon, to look askance. Envy is the sin of an evil eye. No
wonder Dante pictures those guilty of envy in purgatory as
having their eyes sewn shut with iron thread.

## II

How can we define it? Buechner says of envy: "Envy is the
consuming desire to have everybody as unsuccessful as you
are."[2] That is only half of it. Envy is the sorrow at another's
success and the joy over another's misfortune. What is uglier
or more perverse than the face that turns sad and bitter when
another has good fortune or that smiles when another one
fails? Envy turns Paul's instruction, "Rejoice with those who
rejoice, weep with those who weep" (Rom. 12:15), upside down.
We rejoice when others weep and weep when they rejoice. Or,
in a more subtle form, we cannot rejoice or can only half-
heartedly rejoice when others succeed. Dorothy Sayers says of
envy: "It begins by asking, plausibly: Why should not I enjoy
what others enjoy? and it ends by demanding: Why should
others enjoy what I may not? Envy is the great leveller: if it
cannot level things up, it will level things down."[3]

Envy cannot tolerate anyone better or higher; it is "the consuming desire to have everybody as unsuccessful as you are."

## III

Our culture is rife with envy. Under the guise of justice persons tear down every achievement or work of beauty. Justice seeks to give every person equal opportunity for accomplishment; envy despises anyone who accomplishes more. Henry Fairlie says: We seem no longer able to admire, respect or be grateful for what is nobler or lovelier or greater than ourselves. We must pull down—or put down—what is exceptional.[4] And Fairlie identifies a cultural symbol of envy: The gossip column. Such columns all provoke our envy at celebrities and vent our envy by telling us the dark side of celebrities. No one is allowed to remain on a pedestal.

That is a symbol for envy. It casts a shadow on a person's goodness or success. A mark of our envious age is that we look for the worst in everybody. A good person must be repressing a seamy underside; a good deed must have an ulterior motive; a good marriage has to have hidden strains; a successful businessman must be cheating somebody.

Envy is all about us.

## IV

Every sin is a perversion of the good. So is there not a good kind of envy? Some have spoken of a "holy envy" that makes us strive for spiritual gain. We see another whose life is what we would like ours to be and we seek to be like them.

You might be asking, what about ambition? Is all ambition bad? Isn't ambition fueled by envy? There is a sadness over not having another's gifts or accomplishments which can work as an impetus to excellence and achievement. This is not the sin of envy. How can it be a sin to want to do better or be better? But it is a sin when you turn bitter at another's accomplishment and seek to pull them down in order to hoist yourself up.

And there is that sad, wistful envy that looks at another wishing to be like them. That is not the dark sin of envy. But it can become a sin as you turn to self-despising in their presence, when their accomplishment makes your feel worthless.

You may not seek to pull them down but you may avoid them or find it impossible to affirm them and like them.

So there is a good ambition that helps you strive for excellence and there is a sad wistful longing that wishes for what another has or is. But as Dante warned us, "Envy bloweth up men's sighs"[5] and this ambition or wistful longing may be blown up by envy into a despising of others that seeks to pull them down or a self-despising that pushes the self down.

William F. Buckley, Jr. instructs us:

> The line between envy and admiration is slender but it is a Great Wall, and on one side of it is the capital sin, on the other is the generosity of spirit that distinguishes the mother who delights in her daughter's beauty and nourishes her son's talent from the mother who, envying what she does not have and cannot acquire, disdains, or disparages, or despises, and so stunts goodness and excellence.[6]

You see how envy can be deadly not only to others but also to the self.

## V

Of course the Bible warns against envy from Genesis to Revelation. Often envy is placed as the second of the deadly sins, following biblical chronology. Pride was the first sin, ending in expulsion from the Garden. Envy was the second sin, leading to Cain's murder of Abel. Next, Joseph's brothers envied him and plotted to kill him. Then one of the most dramatic stories of envy: "Saul eyed David." The people sang "Saul has slain his thousands, and David his ten thousands." Saul heard, and then "Saul eyed David" (1 Sam. 18:7-9). That envy led Saul to try to kill David. The story goes on. No wonder that George Truett called Envy "incipient murder."

Envy is also bad because it leads to coveting (as in "Thou shalt not covet") which causes unhappiness of spirit and may lead to unworthy means of trying to acquire what you covet. (See the Ten Commandments, Ex. 20:17.)

## VI

Envy has many faces. Perhaps the most prevalent is "professional jealousy." Long ago Aristotle said that "Envy is worst among equals," those who are like you in class, knowledge, and stature.[7] Was Aristotle not right? Saul was not envious of David's harp playing. But when David donned his armor, became a warrior, and slew his ten thousands to Saul's thousands, then "Saul eyed David."

A doctor is not apt to envy a violinist as much as a fellow surgeon. Preachers are apt to be most envious of other preachers. When I was a student I would sit and listen to preachers who came to seminary to preach. Envy would crawl in. Before I had left the service I had rearranged the sermon, switched a few illustrations, corrected the grammar, made proper theological critique, and shortened it by an average of five minutes. The judgment of God on my envy was to call me to Crescent Hill Baptist Church, a church on the edge of a seminary campus with many seminary students. My pulpit is my penance. The justice of the Lord is surely terrible!

Since Cain and Abel, sibling rivalry has been a frequent face of this envy among equals. It arises from the yearning for parental blessing. When parents favor one child and withhold blessing from one, a nursery is set up for envy. Such favoritism provokes envy. A certain amount of competition is healthy among siblings but how unfortunate when a sibling has to compete for the parental blessing or seeks to wrest it from the other. Sibling rivalry may be a paradigm for all envy: Hankering after the blessing given to others, disparaging the blessing given to us.

Envy expresses itself in many ways but one of its favorite tools is the tongue. The artist Giotto, a friend of Dante, painted envy with enlarged ears to catch any breath of rumor or scandal and a serpent tongue to poison a person's reputation. When I lived in New York City, frequently some young hoodlums would see a new Cadillac on the street, take a lead pipe and carve a deep scratch from one end of the car to another—out

of envy. Those of us who wouldn't dream of doing that to somebody's car often think nothing of defacing another's reputation.

So gossip and backbiting have long been noted as chief ex-
pressions of envy. We can do it in subtle ways. To use Alexand-
er Pope's knowing phrase, we "damn with faint praise" those
whom we envy. Listen to an example from Chaucer's Parson—
how contemporary medieval England sounds: "A man praises
his neighbor with a wicked intention, for he puts always a
wicked twist into it at the end. Always he puts a but in at the
end, which implies more blame than all the praise is worth."[8]

Envy is certainly deadly. It destroys us. Joseph Parker, the
great nineteenth-century London preacher, said of envy:
"Beware of envy . . . it is relentless, it will plague your life, it
will rob every flower of its perfume, it will ban the light out of
every window in the house; your dinner today will be no re-
freshment to you." Envy robs life of all its sweetness. It is
endless disparagement of others; it is endless disparagement of
self.

## VII

Now we come to why it is an obstacle to grace. Envy is a
denial of the goodness of God. It wishes to deny God's goodness
to others and refuses to recognize God's goodness to oneself.
Take Jesus' parable of the workers and the hours. Remember,
the master recruited workers at 6 AM, 9 AM, 12 Noon, 3 PM
and 5 PM, and promised to pay them each a day's wages. Then
at the end of the day, he lined up the workers, paid the ones
hired last first and paid them all the same, a day's wages.

The men hired first, the ones who had worked all day, began
to grumble and murmur—grumbling and murmuring are the
sounds of envy. The master looked into their evil eyes and
asked the most probing of all questions:

"Is your eye evil because I am good?" Are you envious because I am generous? (Matt. 20:15).

When envy sees that God is generous to others, it cannot see
how God is generous to oneself. The grumbling workers refused

to see that the master was good to them by providing a fair day's wage for an honest day's work because they were incensed by the master's "unfair" generosity toward those hired last.

How content we are with what we have in life until we see someone else (no more deserving than we!) enjoying more.

In envy's denial of the goodness of God, its heart knows no gratitude. Its narrow slit eyes can see nothing for which to be thankful. Ingratitude is perhaps a major symptom of the sin of envy.

## VIII

What can deliver us from envy? Only a grace stronger than sin, only a love that outlives our envy. The Gospels record that it was "out of envy that [the Jews] had delivered [Jesus] up [for death]" (Matt. 27:18). Jesus bore this sin of ours on the cross. He bore it and bore it away.

Through the infusion of this love of Christ our envy can be overcome. You may wonder if anyone can ever overcome it! It is important with this sin (and all seven) to remember that grace is always at the same time pardon and power. We must receive pardon, for all of us are guilty and only pardon can remove our guilt. But pardon is not enough or we would be in a hopeless circle of sin, repentance, forgiveness, sin, repentance, forgiveness, over and over again. So grace comes as love's power to deliver us from the grip of Envy. In this life we will never perfectly arrive. Grace can deliver us from envy's terrible possession, but it cannot deliver us from its presence. Envy always crouches at the door, and just when we are most unsuspecting it will creep in. So we are yet again in need of pardon. Always, every day we are in need of grace's power *and* pardon.

I hope as you read this chapter you will seek love's power to chase the bitter heart of envy from your spirit and its evil eye from your face. Seek grace to rejoice in God's goodness given to others and to you. Andrew Bonar, a saint of a minister, entered in his diary these words:

This day twenty years ago, I preached for the first time as an ordained minister. It is amazing that the Lord has spared me and used me at all. . . . Yet envy is my hurt and today I have been seeking grace to rejoice exceedingly over the usefulness of others, even where it casts me into the shade. . . . Lord, give more and more to those brothers whom I have despised.[9]

This is true spiritual wisdom: Seek grace to rejoice exceedingly in the usefulness, the beauty, the success, the intelligence of others even when it casts you in the shade. Pray for them to receive even more. That prayer itself will be a healing evidence of grace.

Grace has that kind of power. From Titus we hear a "true saying":

We were slaves to passions and pleasures of all kinds. We spent our lives in malice and envy. . . . But when the kindness and love of God . . . was revealed, he saved us. It was not because of any good deeds that we ourselves had done, but because of his own mercy that he saved us, through the Holy Spirit, who gives us new birth and new life by washing us (Titus 3:3-6, GNB).

May it be so with you and me.

## Notes

1. Chaucer, p. 516.
2. Buechner, p. 20.
3. Sayers, p. 771.
4. Fairlie, p. 64.
5. Dante, *Purgatory,* Canto IV.
6. William F. Buckley, Jr., "The Evils of Envy" in "A Modern Guide to the Seven Deadly Sins" *Esquire,* July 1986 (vol. 106, no. 1) p. 61.
7. Rhetoric II, 10, 1387b-22.
8. Chaucer, p. 516.
9. Quoted in Norman Macleod Caie, *The Seven Deadly Sins* (New York: George H. Doran Company, 1923), p. 29.

SPEAK, IF VERY ANGRY, AN HUNDRED • BE

ANGRY BUT DO NOT SIN, DO NOT LET

THE SUN GO DOWN ON YOUR ANGER •

WHEN ANGRY, COUNT TEN BEFORE YOU

ANGER
the devil's furnace

# 5
# Anger

Frederick Buechner says of anger:

> Of the Seven Deadly Sins, anger is possibly the most fun. To lick
> your wounds, to smack your lips over grievances long past, to
> roll over your tongue the prospect of bitter confrontations still
> to come, to savor to the last toothsome morsel both the pain you
> are given and the pain you are giving back—in many ways it is
> a feast fit for a king. The chief drawback is that what you are
> wolfing down is yourself. The skeleton at the feast is you.[1]

That, as the saying goes, is a mouthful. If anger is fun and
revenge is sweet, it is also a deadly feast.

Anger is pictured in tones of red. In a cartoon if anyone gets
mad they also turn red. The primitive and picturesque Hebrew
language has two words for anger. The first word is to have
"pregnant nostrils." When you act angry the nostrils enlarge.
The same Hebrew word is used for nose and anger. The famous
phrase describing God as "slow to anger" (Ex. 34:6) literally
means to be "long of nose." The other word means "to burn"
or to "grow hot." We think of anger in degrees of heat as well
as tones of red. We use phrases like "boiling mad" or "hothead-
ed" or "flaming temper." No wonder that in *The Canterbury
Tales,* the Parson called anger the "Devil's furnace."[2]

What about an animal for anger? Many have been used: a
toad, pig, rat, rooster, donkey, bull. But none predominate.
Why? Perhaps because the creature that most typifies anger is,

as one has suggested, "a figure riding on a camel, the most vicious of animals."[3] Is not humankind the only animal that harbors hatred and kills simply for sport?

How can we picture anger? In an ancient painting by Pieter Brueghel, dated 1558, anger is pictured with a knife in its mouth, a vial of poison in one hand while the other hand is in a sling, injured in previous battles. Anger is deadly.

# I

There are many types of anger. There is the *powder-keg* kind of anger—the Woody Hayes kind. The famous Ohio State football coach got so mad when a Clemson player intercepted a pass late in a bowl game that he slugged him—at the same moment tendering his resignation. There is the *crock pot* kind of anger. It simmers and stews all day long. There is the anger of *frustration.* This is the special anger of mothers and golfers. What is a mother to do when the child has turned over his glass of milk for the fifth time? And as one golf pro said: "Some people ought never to play golf; it does them more harm than good."

One form of anger celebrated today is *ideological* anger. This is the anger adopted by political or social philosophy when it neatly labels the good guys and the bad, oppressors and the oppressed. A person is no longer a person but a capitalist or Communist or male chauvinist pig or honkie. This ideological anger may fly into violent rage as in the case of the Symbionese Liberation Army or the Ku Klux Klan or the Manson Family. Charles Manson's helter-skelter philosophy was an ideological tract of hatred against rich white people.

This ideological anger is a mutant strain of what the biblical tradition knows as "righteous wrath." The "Wrath of God" is the purifying and rectifying righteousness of God directed against wickedness. God uses historical forces and persons as instruments of His righteousness, a righteousness that sets things right. Often these human instrumentalities do not even know they are so being used. Assyria was used by God in Old

Testament times as the "rod" of His wrath. the Psalmist has a phrase, "The wrath of men shall praise thee" (Ps. 76:10). Sometimes it can.

However, we must be most careful when we see ourselves as instruments of God's righteous wrath. Our righteous indignation too often turns to unrighteous vindictiveness. While calling righteous indignation a "good anger," Chaucer's Parson warns that it must be "gentle and without bitterness."

Indeed Dorothy Sayers says that her British kinfolk are particularly susceptible to the dangers of righteous indignation. She described this sin:

> He would rather the evil were not cured at all than it were cured quietly and without violence. His evil lust of wrath cannot be sated unless somebody is hounded down, beaten, and trampled on and a savage war-dance executed upon the body.[4]

I would offer this one guideline about righteous indignation. Anger at injustice is one of the sources of energy God gives us to fight for justice. It turns from virtue into vice, however, when we become as evil as the evil we fight. When we become like the enemy in order to defeat the enemy, what have we gained? Our means must be as pure and righteous as our ends. That is one difference between ideological anger and righteous wrath: The latter uses means consistent with the kingdom of God.

If anger has many types it expresses itself in many ways. It is a knife in the mouth: Sarcasm (literally, to tear the flesh), cursing, and slander. It may erupt in violence, physical or psychological violence. It can take passive forms of expression (what psychology calls passive-aggressive behavior): You give somebody the "silent treatment"; you withhold affection; you refuse to enter into the party with enthusiasm; you show up late; you decide not to clean the house; you drag your feet on a project of work.

## II

Our society has elevated some forms of anger to the status of a virtue. Under the cloak of honesty we are coached to vent our anger. (Sad isn't it that when someone says, "May I be honest with you," we automatically duck for cover. Why can't honesty ever be an opportunity to say something good!) A cartoon pictured a living room in absolute shambles. The wife is saying to her husband, "I think it is wonderful to be so direct with your anger." A character in an Andre Dubus novella describes some women who have been to a women's divorce support group: "They met with women's groups, shrank each other's heads without a professional in the room, and came away with their anger so prodded they were like warriors."[5] Today we proudly claim our anger and level it at the poor person we think is responsible for our hurt. "Let It All Hang Out" goes the popular slogan, but in fact bad temper is a form of public littering. As Willard Gaylin says: "that Out in which you are choosing to let It hang is mine as well as yours!" So he counsels us to "keep It in."[6]

There is a popular assumption about that every suppressed emotion is an unhealthy emotion, which derives, says Gaylin, from "a sloppy reading of early Freud." Carol Tavris takes on this popular assumption in her book *Anger: The Misunderstood Emotion.*[7] Sometimes, she says, suppressed anger is good for you; it used to be called common courtesy:

> Our contemporary ideas about anger have been fed by the anger industry, psychotherapy, which too often is based on the belief that inside every tranquil soul a furious one is screaming to get out. Psychiatric theory refers to anger as if it were a fixed amount of energy that bounces through the system: if you pinch it here it is bound to pop out there—in bad dreams, neurosis, hysterical paralyses, hostile jokes, or stomachaches.[8]

Why do we, she asks, resist the idea that we can control our emotions? Seneca the Stoic had as good an answer as any: "Because we are in love with our vices; we uphold them and prefer to make excuses for them rather than shake them off.[9]

We would be fools not to recognize the merit in the psychological truth that too much suppressed anger can lead to problems, not the least of which is depression or ulcers. As the pundit said: You can swallow more anger than you can digest. But Tavris and Gaylin argue that we have carried this truth too far and used it simplistically.

Indiscriminate vented anger is a social event introducing a new social situation which may itself create a spiral toward more anger. "Any emotional arousal will eventually simmer down," advises Tavris, "if you just wait long enough."[10] Such is wisdom behind the classic device of counting to ten. "When angry, count ten before you speak; if very angry, an hundred" (Thomas Jefferson). The actress Lynn Fontaine once said that the secret of her successful marriage to Alfred Lunt was that they were never impolite to each other.[11] How refreshing that comment sounds.

Perhaps the first thing we should consider, then, is that the popular wisdom that urges us, for our health's sake, to express our anger may not be all its cracked up to be. Anger is not a virtue but one of the seven deadly sins.

### III

How do we begin to get a handle on the problem of anger? Popular wisdom says vent it. Christians have long been taught to "swallow it."

What are we to do with it? How can we deal responsibly with anger? First, we need to make the distinction the apostle Paul made: "Be angry but do not sin" (Eph. 4:26). The impulse of anger is not in and of itself a sin. It is the handling of that anger that turns it into a sin.

Look at the physiology of anger. When you get angry the pulse rate quickens, the blood sugar goes up, the anticoagulants decrease. Anger is nature's defense package; it is getting you ready for fight or for flight. It has been aptly called by psychoanalyst Sandor Rado one of our "emergency emotions."

Anger is our response to threat, whether the threat be disapproval, betrayal, deprivation, exploitation and manipulation, frustration, violence, or humiliation.[12] The key issue however is that in human beings anger is not for long just a natural impulse. It begins to join with human faculties of mind and spirit. Our ability to step back and take a look at ourselves and our world (what philosophers name our self-trancendence) is blessing and curse. Our perspective on life can help us cope with threat or it can in fact manufacture anger so that this anger becomes a deadly poison. It is not a sin to experience anger flaring up in the presence of threat, but we have the capacity to keep anger's pot boiling long after the threat is gone. For any number of reasons, we keep the anger hot. Some people are angry all the time. And often we vent this anger on the wrong persons.

Or, something else happens, our anger impulse turns from hot to cold and becomes a brooding, resentful anger which festers and infects the spirit. When such things happen, anger becomes a sin.

One way to define the deadly sin called anger is this: The irresponsible management of anger. What does the responsible management of anger look like? Here are some brief guidelines.

(1) Accept your anger (own up to it); (2) learn to understand it; and (3) express it directly, if appropriate, to the person(s) involved. This is not an untempered venting of your anger which often will make matters worse. When is direct expression of anger appropriate? After you have taken the time to cool down and to reflect on your anger and understand it sufficiently well to know that, in fact, the other person bears some responsibility for the hurt. Then not only will your expression of it be appropriate but also the manner of your expression will be emotionally appropriate to the size of the hurt. This procedure follows the advice of Jesus: "If your brother sins against you, go and tell him his fault, between you and him alone" (Matt. 18:15). If you find yourself unable to manage your anger

without destructive consequences, then taking responsibility might mean going to a counselor or therapist.

Irresponsible management of anger is on one extreme the destructive venting of anger, a venting which far from dissipating the anger revs it up for more. The other extreme is ignoring or swallowing your anger which results, as Andrew Lester explains in his helpful book *Coping with Anger: A Christian Guide,* in the loss of control over that anger. "That which we suppress we lose control over."[13] Irresponsible management of anger leads to its becoming a deadly sin.

## IV

The deadly sin of anger is not the impulse of anger. It is the form of anger that begins to organize the self around itself. Our selfhood becomes focused on anger, vengeance, hatred, resentment. This form of anger is not just a sin against another person and against the self. It is also a sin against God. It is an obstacle to grace. We need to see it in this dimension before we can seek and find help from beyond.

The deadly sin of anger (as envy) denies the goodness of God. It says, "I deserve more" and keeps angrily focused on what "I do not have." Anger is also a denial of the justice of God. The vengeful person seeks to take God's place at the throne of judgment. It is no accident that when Paul warns us against vengeful actions he closes his argument with the words:

> Leave it to the wrath of God; for it is written "Vengeance is mine, I will repay, says the Lord." No, "if your enemy is hungry, feed him, if he is thirsty, give him drink. . . ." Do not be overcome by evil, but overcome evil with good (Rom. 12:19-21).

We cannot justify revenge, for revenge refuses to trust in the final justice and righteousness of God. Our concern for justice is never pure; it is subtly entangled in vindictiveness. We cannot "get even." Only in God's hand is justice safe and sure, "For in him it is held in an eternity of Holy Love."[14]

Vengeance is a denial of the justice of God. Freedom from

anger owns our anger then yields our anger to God. It makes its complaint to God and then leaves it with God.[15]

But that is not the only way anger is an obstacle to grace. It not only denies God's justice, it refuses God's forgiveness.

Jesus offers us the impossible command—"Love your enemies" (Matt. 5:44). Theologian Karl Barth defined the "enemy" as anyone who tempts you to return evil for evil. That enemy can be as intimate as a spouse and as nearby as a boss. The command to love your enemy is possible only with the miracle of forgiveness. As with every command of God, God gives us the power to fulfill it. The forgiveness of God is the source of our forgiveness. Your forgiveness of someone who has hurt you is rarely an instantaneous accomplishment. More often it is a step-by-step process, like retracing your steps out of a blind alley.[16]

The issue of forgiveness becomes spiritually crucial because we can not fully receive God's forgiveness while withholding it from another. Grace given to you is always on its way to someone else. To stop it is to block it from your own life. Forgiveness comes into our lives by way of a double-hinged door. It swings both ways or not at all. When we block the outgo we stop the inflow.

Anger is an awesome obstacle to grace because as we withhold grace from another we keep it from ourselves. That is why Jesus taught us to pray "Forgive us our debts as we also have forgiven our debtors." Anger is such an obstacle to grace that Jesus says we cannot even worship while holding a grudge. So He commanded:

"So if you are offering your gift at the altar, and there remember that your brother has something against you, leave your gift there before the altar and go; first be reconciled to your brother, and then come and offer your gift" (Matt. 5:23-24).

Jesus' spiritual sensitivity is unerring. We cannot worship God while hating our neighbor. That should be heard as an urgent call for us to do some patching up of bad relationships.

You may begin taking steps this very day. The first step

begins in an inner resolve. The next step is a change of behavior: You act as if the forgiveness is given. You act for the well-being of the other. Pray for the freeing of the heart to forgive that person. The process has begun. The other person may never let reconciliation happen but as you forgive that person, you will be free from the hurts of the past. God wants us to live free from the hurts of the past. That is why He forgives us and calls us to be forgiving of others.

I knew a physician who hated one of his partners. He detested everything about the man and it was chewing him up inside. He decided to pray for that man, thinking that it would be impossible to pray for him and still hate him. And he decided to pray for him everytime he washed his hands, which was fifty to sixty times a day. He tried that formula, but it didn't seem to be working. Finally he burst out to God: "God I hate that man and I need your help."

That is what I mean by owning your anger then yielding it. As the doctor kept praying, the victory was won.

### Conclusion

I call you to a feast, not a feast of anger whose main course is you, but to a feast of forgiveness whose bread is Christ's body and whose cup is His blood. I invite you to the Christ. Augustine once said: "When the winds and waves of angry passion rush upon your soul, do what the disciples did when the tempest fell upon them in the boat. Call to Christ."

Call to Christ. Ask for the gift of forgiveness. Seek love's power to reconcile. His is a power from beyond and yet from deep within our humanness, for Christ's heart which can beat in yours took the full fury of our anger and from that cross cried "Father, forgive."

### Notes

1. *Wishful Thinking*, p. 2.
2. Chaucer, p. 519.

3. Quoted in May, p. 86.

4. Sayers, p. 66-7.

5. Andre Dubus, "Finding a Girl in America" in *We Don't Live Here Anymore* (New York: Crown Publishers, 1984), pp. 238-39.

6. "Putting It Back Where It Belongs," *Hastings Center Report,* February, 1977, p. 22.

7. Carol Tavris, *Anger: The Misunderstood Emotion* (New York: Simon & Schuster, 1982), p. 21.

8. Ibid., p. 61.

9. In Tavris, p. 61.

10. Ibid., p. 122.

11. Reported in Tavris, p. 222.

12. This list is supplied by Willard Gaylin, *The Rage Within: Anger in Modern Life* (New York: Simon & Schuster, 1984).

13. Andrew D. Lester, *Coping with Your Anger: A Christian Guide* (Philadelphia: The Westminister Press, 1983), pp. 52-54; also "Toward a New Understanding of Anger in Christian Experience," *Review and Expositor* Vol. 78, No. 4., pp. 563-90. See also David and Vera Mace, *How to Have a Happy Marriage* (Nashville: Abingdon, 1977), pp. 97-130.

14. The phrase is George Arthur Buttrick's taken from an unpublished lecture.

15. See Psalm 109 and also Walter Brueggemann's chapter "Vengeance—Human and Divine in his *Praying the Psalms* (Winona, Minn.: Saint Mary's Press, 1982).

16. Lewis Smedes, *Forgive and Forget* (San Francisco: Harper & Row, 1984). This book is a remarkable guide to the process of forgiveness.

...the love of possessing
that orders the self around possessions
and closes its eye
to the neighbor...
GREED
THE LOVE OF MONEY
IS THE ROOT OF ALL EVIL;

THEIR HEART WITH MANY PANGS

AWAY FROM THE FAITH AND PIERCED

THAT SOME HAVE WANDERED

IT IS THROUGH THIS CRAVING

# 6
# Avarice

Tolstoy told a story of a man who was told that he could have as much land as he could run around in one day. He set off to encircle his plot of land. As the day wore on the circle got larger and larger. Compelled by the thought of all the land he would own he kept widening the circumference of the circle, stride by stride, mile by mile, until at sunset he staggered and dropped dead of a heart attack. His story is the story of avarice, of persons and nations run to death by greed.

## I

Sin is a distortion of the good, a fact most poignantly true as we study the last three deadly sins—greed, gluttony, and lust. In each something which in its proper measure is good turns bad as it becomes the center around which the self is organized: In greed possessions, in gluttony food and drink, and in lust sex.

"Beware of coveteousness," Jesus said. Two brothers had come to Jesus seeking a judge to settle their inheritance squabble. I will not preside over your greed, Jesus answered, and with that warning against greed He told a parable about a rich fool (Luke 12:13-21, KJV).

The deadly sin we encounter in this chapter is avarice—variously called greed, or covetousness. The various Sins are associated with different parts of the human anatomy: Pride's camel nose or swollen chest, anger's flared nostrils and red face, the evil eye of envy. Avarice has to do with the arms and hands: the grasping hand, the tight fist. In Moliere's play on avarice, the greedy hero has the name "harpagon" derived from the Latin *harpe* which means claw or sickle.[1] With avarice, arms and hands are turned into grappling hooks.

So maybe an octopus is the most appropriate animal. And gray might be the color, cold, steel gray. Color avarice cold. In Dorothy Sayers' grouping of sins into the three warm-hearted and disrespectable sins (lust, gluttony, and anger) and the four cold hearted and respectable sins (pride, sloth, envy, and avarice),[2] avarice is coldhearted. (Anger, I would argue, can be either hot or cold, but the colder it gets, the worse it gets; so also the law argues as it distinguishes between crimes of passion and cold-blooded murder.) Jesus' words were, in general, much harder on the cold-hearted sins and His warnings against greed were especially stern.

## II

Greed is a deadly sin so we dare not treat it lightly. We live within powerful structures of greed and we ourselves so easily become greedy. In the Gospels Jesus talked more about money than any other single subject except the kingdom of God (which was the subject behind everything He taught). It gives one the impression Jesus knew what a subtle destroyer greed was. We take it less seriously than Jesus at our own peril. Remember greed prevented the rich young ruler from following Jesus. He turned sadly away "for he was very rich" (Luke 18:23).

Some of you may want to skip this chapter after its rather forbidding beginning. For these, allow me to emphasize that freedom from greed which comes as a gift of the gospel can transform your existence and make you strangely (it may seem to your mind now) joyful.

## III

How might we picture avarice today? The old picture of avarice is of the miser, shut up in his hiding place, running his fingers through his coins. A Scrooge. As a young boy I was introduced to this kind of person through Donald Duck's uncle: Scrooge McDuck.

But like most sins today, avarice has come out of the closet. What used to be a vice now parades glamorously as a virtue. American life is turned into a TV game show called "Conspicuous Consumption." Million-dollar-ad campaigns provoke our covetousness, pumping products we don't need, creating in us the desire for things we wouldn't otherwise even know about. Credit cards facilitate our avarice, plastic money tempting us to buy things which satisfy equally artificial wants. The question every Christmas is: What do you buy the man who has everything and is still paying for it?

Professional sports have regular strikes—out of greed. Washington, D.C., our seat of government, has become an exclusive club for millionaires where a main agenda is to protect the wealthy. Just ask David Stockman how "Reaganomics" was scuttled by self-interest groups: "The hogs were feeding. The greed level . . . just got out of control."[3] Illegal drug sales tempt thousands of Americans from teenagers up to enter the drug economy with the lure of easy money. Cocaine becomes a white plague. The comedian Robin Williams said it well: "Cocaine is God's way of saying, 'You have too much money.' " *Newsweek* reports that the marijuana crop is a billion-dollar-a-year business in America. These are signs of an affluent society sick with greed.

And the church is not free from guilt. Throughout history we have had hucksters of the gospel who sell the free grace of God for personal gain. *Simony* is the name we give to the enterprise of selling spiritual rewards (from the figure of Simon in Acts 8:18).

In Chaucer's *The Canterbury Tales,* the Pardoner tells a morality play about greed. Three men find a chest of gold. One of them goes to bring back wine and bread for supper. While he is away the other two plot to kill him. When he arrives they do him in. But the deceased has already poisoned the wine. They drink it and die. All three lie dead at the foot of their treasure, killed by greed.

Then after telling the story, the Pardoner offers to forgive anyone of their sins—including, of course, greed—if they will pay the appropriate fee! TV preachers spend a large measure of their TV time asking for money; and no wonder, it takes fifty cents of every dollar raised to pay for the TV time which they use to raise money for more TV time.

Today simony is practiced in more sophisticated ways. The Pope sold indulgences in Luther's day and such corruption helped spur the Reformation. We sell "seed-faith" today: "Seed-faith can heal your pocketbook!" Or, we make God our business partner: "Love God and Get Rich!" Some people's pocketbooks are particularly vulnerable to spiritual shysters and preachers are tempted to build their own kingdoms rather than God's.

Alfred Lord Tennyson must have seen such shenanigans in his day for in his poem "Sea Dreams" he described a person:

> . . . with the fat affectionate smile
> That makes the widow lean . . .
>
> ................................................................................
> Who, never naming God except for gain,
> So never took that useful name in vain,
> Made Him his catspaw and the Cross
> his tool,
> And Christ the bait to trap his dupe
> and fool.[4]

How terrible to sell God's grace for gain, or to use the gospel as an appeal to our Greed!

Let us now move, more personally.

## IV

We can well understand greed as a compulsion of the false self. It is the compulsion to fill the emptiness of self with things. It lives by the false truth: You are what you own.

Avarice can take the form of compulsive spending. We feel good only when we are buying things. The way to escape the blues is to go to the mall and buy something. "When the going gets tough, the tough go shopping." Moreover, the credit-card business makes compulsive spending an easy route to financial slavery—at 16 to 25 percent interest per year. A story is told of a girl telling her boyfriend, "My mom is happy only when she is spending money. She went shopping every day until thieves stole her credit cards." "Did your dad report the theft?" asked the boyfriend. "No," replied the girl, "the thieves are spending less than my mom did."

Avarice can also take the course of compulsive nonspending —in the case of the miser. A person spends far less than he owns so he can build a secure nest egg. Some children of the Great Depression have become compulsive nonspenders, saving every penny against the threat of disaster. No amount of money ever makes them feel secure.

Compulsive is the way of the false self. It compulsively works, saves, spends. Henri Nouwen says that the two main enemies of the spiritual life are the twin compulsions of anger and greed. He explains about greed: ". . . where my sense of self depends on what I can acquire, greed flares up when my desires are frustrated.[5]

Have you ever gone into a pout when you couldn't buy what you wanted? How many hours do you spend looking through the want-ads, dreaming of what you want next? Ever lost a night's sleep fretting over something you wanted to buy? What would you be willing to do to get those things you want? These are some of the compulsions of the false self called greed.

### IV

We are moving closer to a definition of greed. Greed is the love of possessing that orders the self around possessions and closes its eye to the neighbor.

The apostle Paul calls covetousness an idolatry (Col. 3:5). The self orders itself around things rather than God. Dante pictures in "Purgatory" those who are guilty of avarice. They are stretched face down on the ground, repeating the words of the psalmist, "My soul cleaveth to the dust" (119:25, KJV). The poet Browning once said, "A spark disturbs our clod." Avarice ignores the divine spark and clings to the clod.

The Bible warns against greed all through its pages. The Tenth Commandment pertains: "Thou shalt not covet" (Ex. 20:17, KJV). The prophets, sobbing with God's own tears, decried the sin of greed which lured Israel and Judah. Jeremiah saw the fall of Judah linked to their enslavement to greed. "From the least to the greatest," he said, "every one is greedy for unjust gain" (8:10). The wise writer of Proverbs asked to be spared both riches and poverty, lest in riches he be full, deny God, and say "Who is the Lord?" or lest in poverty he steal and curse God's name (Prov. 30:7-9).

All through the Bible there is the suggestion that the more we get, the more we keep and the less we give to the helpless. That truth is substantiated statistically. People with incomes below $10,000 give three times more proportionally to charities than people with incomes $50,000-$100,000, and people with incomes below $50,000 give almost twice as much proportionally as people in the $100,000 to $200,000 category.[6] It is no wonder that Jesus said, "How hard it is for those who have riches to enter the kingdom of God! For it is easier for a camel to go through the eye of a needle than for a rich man to enter the kingdom of God" (Luke 18:24-25).

Paul warns us with these words: "The love of money is the root of all evils; it is through this craving that some have wandered away from the faith and pierced their hearts with many pangs" (1 Tim. 6:10).

## V

The way of Jesus leads us to some answers. His life was the joyful way of a man who found His sufficiency in God. He enjoyed good things which life offered, but His life was not organized around the accumulation of things. He warned of the danger of riches to lure us away from God and neighbor. Take His parable of the rich fool: The rich man is a fool because he forgets that all he has is a gift from God and assumes that his riches are his (Luke 12:16-21).

Observe the pronouns in the rich fool's speech: I, I, my, I, I, my, I, my, my, I, my, myself, self. Thirteen out of sixty-one words refer to I, me, mine.

The man is totally self-absorbed. Sitting in splendid isolation, he says to himself: "Self, you have ample goods, take it easy, eat, drink and be merry." The fool is stuck in the first-person singular. No thought of neighbor or of God. Greed turns us into strangers in paradise, strangers to God, to self, and to neighbor.

The fool's solution to the situation of abundance is not to share but to store. That betrays the state of his soul.

The verdict of God is sharp: "Fools! This night your soul is required of you" (v. 20). Death mocks the terrible illusion of greed that our possessions offer us any real security. Death marks the final failure of things; they cannot bring us happiness.

## VI

Greed is an obstacle to grace in a most serious way. We are stewards of God's grace, and this refers to material blessings as well as spiritual blessings. Greed blocks the free flow of God's earth gifts to His children. Creation and all its fruits belong to all God's children. Greed dams up the free flow of the wealth of God's land so only a few can enjoy.

A biblical theology of stewardship is the antidote of avarice. Here is a short theology of stewardship: Our material possessions are not divine to be worshiped. They are not evil to be despised. They are God's good gifts to be used for the glory of God.

A proper concept of stewardship recognizes both the goodness of material things and also their limitation. They are good but not *The Good*. God gives us material things to enjoy, but when our desire to have things becomes a compulsion and the neighbor is ignored then it becomes the sin of Avarice. To recognize the goodness of material things keeps us from becoming ascetic and renouncing God's good gifts as evil; to recognize the limitation of material things keeps us from fashioning them into idols.

Jesus' way was not the way of an ascetic—He enjoyed life and accepted an occasional extravagance. Neither was His way that of a materialist—He warned against mammon's idolatry. His way was the way of generosity—a thankful and free receiving *and* giving of God's good gifts. The hands of asceticism are held palm up in refusal. The hands of materialism are grasping and closed. The way of Jesus is a third way, the way of generosity, hands open, gratefully receiving and freely giving.

I like the way a good suit feels on my body; I like to wax a shiny car; I like the smell of leather and the polished grain of wood in finely crafted furniture; I like a spacious home with enough room. But there is a point in life when these likes become compulsions and these wants dull my vision of my neighbor's need. The Bible does not say "Despise these material blessings," but it does say "Do not worship them, do not hoard them, do not depend upon them." Another way of saying it is: Sit loose with your possessions. Paul pointed to this when he said, let those who buy "buy as though they had no goods. . . . For the form of this world is passing away" (1 Cor. 7:30-31).

How do we buy as if we do not own? We sit loose with them. We do not let our possessions become too dear. We do not let them interfere with our vocation as a Christian to love God with all our being and to love our neighbor as ourself.

This sitting loose with things is more than a step for self-improvement—though it will enhance your selfhood. It is more than a Stoic distance on all things which in their fateful fickleness may be here today and gone tomorrow. It is a call to be rich in the kingdom of God.

Store up riches where it counts, Jesus said. Store up riches that cannot be taken away. Store up riches in heaven. The word *heaven* refers to far more than a place in the hereafter where we will receive "stars in our crown." It stands for the kingdom of God which is alive here and now as well as in the final realm of God.

The kingdom of God is the care for the needy. It is the just distribution of God's earth-gifts to all His children. The kingdom of God is a banquet where all are invited. The kingdom of God is the spreading of peace, the protection of God's creation, the establishment of justice, and the free gift of joy to all God's creatures. Greed hinders the kingdom, generosity enhances it.

Storing up treasures in heaven is the investment of our lives in something that matters, in the kingdom of God rather than in the enthralling kingdoms of this world. A theology of stewardship challenges greed which blocks God's grace; it helps that grace and its earth gifts flow.

## VII

Christ offers you more, however, than a good theology of stewardship. He offers a grace that is pardon and power.

No one should languish in guilty conscience. How do we in affluent America find peace in God's hand when we live in a world of so much hunger and poverty and injustice? Our consciences stay troubled.

Here God offers us the pardon of grace. It is not deserved. None of us have done all we could do, or ever will. We live by the mercy of God. Grace's pardon is not syrup poured over our waffles; it is not license to do as we please. It is freedom from immobilizing guilt to get on with the kingdom work.

But grace is more than pardon; it is also power. The power of grace brings us gospel simplicity. Gospel simplicity is distinct from the voice of affluence which says, "You are what you own" and from the voice of aceticism which says, "You are what you refuse." It enjoys the goodness of life but is always sharing that goodness with others.

Gospel simplicity gives us freedom from anxiety and freedom for others. Jesus said, "Be not anxious" and the words were as much invitation as command. You don't have to stay anxious

over your economic existence. You can trust in God to take care
of you.

You may scoff at such a simple truth, but if you analyze your
life, most of your economic anxiety comes not at the point of
your basic needs, but in your overspending in pursuit of all
your wants. Or it comes trying to master the future and be
secure against all possible problems. But as the rich fool discovered, storing up things to make us more secure probably makes
us even less secure since there's more to worry about losing.

Jesus offers us freedom from anxiety and freedom from
things so that we can be free for others. Gospel simplicity helps
us be of one heart and mind about that. You don't have to worry
so much if your life is in order, if you are not overreaching
economically, if your security is in the right things.

The grace that can free you is the grace of Jesus Christ. It
comes as you deepen your relationship with Him. It comes as
your lives center more and more in Him, as you develop what
Thomas A. Kempis called a "familiar friendship with Jesus."[7]
This familiar friendship is the deepening of Christ's Spirit in
yours. As we develop this friendship we begin to hear His voice
more clearly above all the other voices of the world. We experience a grace that frees us from the compulsions of this world.
A favorite verse from Psalm 37 (v. 4) goes: "Delight thyself also
in the Lord; and he shall give thee the desires of thine heart."
This is not promise of a blank check. Carlyle Marney has translated it this way: Delight thyself in the Lord and he will teach
your heart what you can afford to want. Christ can change your
"wanter." The way of gospel simplicity does not offer a new
legalism, trading one compulsiveness for another. Rather, life
in Christ issues into the joyful opening of the heart and hand
to God and to neighbor.

The grace of the Lord Jesus Christ will give you peace in the
hand of God; it will set you free from anxiety of the heart and
make you rich in the kingdom of God.

I began this chapter with Tolstoy's story of greed. I close with
another image. A man had a dream wherein he went first to

hell and then to heaven. When he passed through hell he saw that everyone had their arms fastened straight in splints from shoulders to fingertips. Tables all around were filled with the most sumptuous food, but they were all starving because they could not get their hands to their mouths.

Then the man traveled to heaven where he saw everyone in the same condition, arms straightened in splints. However, in heaven everyone was happy and filled for they were feeding each other.

The way of greed keeps us in splendid isolation; alone we live and alone we die. The way of generosity which is the way of gospel simplicity[8] makes us rich in the kingdom of God, for it gives to us community. Your life can be richer as Christ frees you from things and frees you for others.

## Notes

1. May, p. 52
2. Sayers, pp. 64 f.
3. William Greider, "The Education of David Stockman," *The Atlantic Monthly*, Dec. 1981, Vol. 248, no. 6, p. 51.
4. *The Poems of Tennyson* (Cambridge: The Riverside Press, 1898), pp. 254-55.
5. Henri Nouwen, *The Way of the Heart* (New York: The Seabury Press, 1981), p. 23.
6. Reported by Brian O'Connell, founding President of Independent Sector, a national coalition of 650 foundations, corporations, and volunteer organizations that promote charities and voluntary organizations, *USA Today*, Wednesday, August 13, 1986, p. 7A.
7. *The Imitation of Christ*, Second Book, chapter VIII.
8. I have expanded on the way of gospel simplicity in "The Working Minister's Lifestyle: Affluence or Simplicity" in *The God-Called Minister*, Morris Ashcraft, editor.

My food is to do the will of him who sent me, and to accomplish his work.

A GLUTTON IS ONE WHO RAIDS THE ICEBOX FOR A CURE FOR SPIRITUAL MALNUTRITION.

# 7
# Gluttony

Last night I got into bed with a Dove Bar. I had had a hard day.
I needed companionship, an understanding presence, a friend.
The ice-cream was a little disappointing. But the chocolate coat-
ing lived completely up to my expectations and hopes for total
fulfillment . . . . Well, it could have been worse. It could have
been unfrozen Sara Lee eclairs, an entire zoo of Gummy Bears,
or guacamole for six.[1]

That is how Wendy Wasserstein began her short essay, "Giving in to Gluttony." On some nights, she concludes, "There's
nothing like a little gluttony." It would be hard to disagree.
What's more enjoyable than a barbecue cookout with friends
when there's far more to eat and drink than you possibly need?
Part of the enjoyment of going to movies is the hot, buttered
popcorn and coke. And some ice creams—they are so creamy
you can almost hear a contented cow moo.

Eating is one of the great delights that God has given us.
What then is the deadly sin called gluttony?

## I

Perhaps I should begin by saying that American culture has
put us in a double bind. We can't win. On one hand you are
being told to eat sumptuously. On the other hand you are being
told to be thin. Everytime you ride down the street or open a
magazine or turn on the TV you are told to eat. Have you

grasped the fact of how many commercials have to do with eating and drinking? On the other hand every glamorous figure on billboards, in magazines, or on TV is about twenty pounds underweight. The symbol of consumption is the sign: "All You Can Eat—$4.98." The symbol of thin mania is the ad: Lose fifty pounds in five weeks. If you look through *Books in Print* you'll see about 200 cookbooks every year.[2] On the other hand, health exercise books and videos have been on the best-seller list for several years.

What a double bind! Culture has its own set of Ten Commandments and chief among them is the commandment: Thou Shalt Not Be Overweight. At the same time you are being told to eat like royalty, you are being told to look like models in *Seventeen* or *Gentlemen's Quarterly*. The teenager's slim body is held up as the ideal which not only demoralizes most of us but also prompts us to unhealthy patterns of starvation and exercise. If you stray from the mark and don't pass the pinch test or inch test, you are given culture's condemnation. How easy it is then to fall into self-despising.

So early on I want you to begin to turn your ears not to culture's voice but to Christ's voice. The good news of Jesus Christ is "in Christ there is no condemnation!" Fat does not damn you. Thin does not save you. No matter what you weigh or what shape you are in, you have infinite worth in God's eyes. You are loved by God, you are accepted by Christ. You are saved by grace, not by good works or good diets. I say this early on because guilt-ridden dieting caused by society's accusing voice ("You must be thin.") or the church's voice ("The devil wants you fat.") rarely leads to healthy, sustained weight loss.

## II

What then is the sin of gluttony? It is the love of consuming food and drink that disrupts your relationship with your body-self, your neighbor, and your God.

Like lust, gluttony is a distortion of the good. Eating is one of God's greatest gifts. Eating is fun. Moreover, as psychoanalysts remind us, eating satisfies not only physical needs but deep psychic needs as well. Oral gratification soothes our battered psyches. Gluttony distorts this pleasure and turns it into compulsion. Gluttony has given food value all out of proportion.

Along with lust, gluttony is one of Sayers' warmhearted sins: "Gluttony is warm-hearted. It is the excess and perversion of that free, careless and generous mood which desires to enjoy life and to see others enjoy it."[3] Warmhearted sins come from lovable and generous hearts. Perhaps that is why Jesus was more tenderhearted toward these kinds of sins. Did you know gluttony was the only one of the seven deadly sins Jesus was directly accused of committing? The Pharisees murmured accusingly: "Behold, a glutton and a drunkard, a friend of tax-collectors and sinners" (Matt. 11:19). They wanted an ascetic, life-despising Christ. Jesus would have none of it, and while He was not a glutton and warned against it, He was not averse to spending time with gluttons. I think He knew warmhearted sinners were closer to the kingdom than coldhearted sinners.

## III

The Bible warns of gluttony early on. Esau sold his birthright to Jacob for a bowl of porridge. The Old Testament word for gluttony means "worthless" and refers to a person who eats and drinks to the point of being worthless. Throughout the Bible gluttony and drunkenness are paired together. Being too full of either dulls the senses. What sad irony that what begins as an effort to please the senses ends in a dulling of the senses.

Orson Wells said once that gluttony is not a private sin, referring to his obvious girth. In fact, it is private, or privatizing. Food is meant to be enjoyed communally, but for the glutton, the world around the table shrinks to "me and my food."

Gluttony has many different faces, many different shapes. One form of gluttony is a preoccupation with food. *Do you eat to live* or *live to eat?* You can order your days around what to eat next.

In the sixth century Gregory the Great spoke of another form of gluttony: *fastidiousness.* Fastidiousness is the paying of undue attention to the planning and preparation of food. The food must be "just so"; it must be a certain brand or kind; it must be cooked just right.

So health-food fanatics may be as gluttonous as junk-food junkies. Endless hours are spent selecting, mixing, and blending. Even dieting can be gluttonous when it becomes obsessive. The dieter may be slimmer of waist but he/she is still living to eat: planning proteins, counting calories, selecting starches, gobbling vitamins, calculating carbohydrates. Who has time for anything else? Still living to eat.

In a "Wizard of Id" comic strip, the preacher preached a sermon on the many virtues of moderation—like most sermons it seemed to go on and on. After the service the king passed by the preacher in the foyer and said: "I think you overdid it." We can even overdo moderation!

America is on a moderation binge called health. Obsession with health has become a multimillion dollar business. Obsessed with looking young and thin, we frantically check our diets and do our exercising. An endless mental exercise is how much can I eat and still not gain weight.

Ours is a compulsive society. Everything we do is to excess— even health. Perhaps a symbol of such a society is that some people overeat to the point of destruction while others suffer from anorexia nervosa and starve themselves, sometimes to the point of death.

## IV

Gluttony distorts our relationship to our body-self. We get caught up in a vain preoccupation with the body, which can lead to an undisciplined feeding of it or a compulsive trimming of it. Or we can despise our body and neglect it.

One answer the Bible gives is a proper theology of the body. One erroneous theology is to idolize the body and cater to its every whim—as if a sign were hung around its neck: "Feed on

Demand." The other erroneous theology is to say the body is evil, bad, demonic, and ignore its needs. The body then is abused or neglected. Some people walk into a room as if their body were the center of the universe; other people sneak into a room pretending their body is invisible, hoping no one will notice. Both are distortions in our relationship to our body-self. Gluttony can come from a worshiping of the body or a despising of it.

The apostle Paul was confronted by both false theologies of the body in Corinth. Some worshiped the body as divine. Others despised it as demonic. Paul rejected both and said: "The body is not divine to be worshipped; the body is not demonic to be despised. The body is the temple of the Holy Spirit—God's good gift to you—to be used to glorify God" (see 1 Cor. 6:19-20).

This theology of the body calls us to a healthy appreciation of the body without an idolization of it. This means first of all that you enjoy it and take care of it. God's health package for you includes: Moderate intake of food and drink, proper rest, and proper exercise. So to start with, take care of your body; do you not know it is God's gift to you—a temple of His Spirit?

However, a healthy appreciation of the body must not become an unhealthy preoccupation with it. Vain pampering, compulsive exercising, daily fretting over inches here and there can become the sin of gluttony. Everyone has their own healthy body weight and shape which they can and should maintain without undue preoccupation. It may not be society's ideal body weight and shape, but very few can fit that.

Your body is the temple of the Holy Spirit to be used for the glory of God. This means that the body must be oriented toward love of God and neighbor. The highest motive for victory over gluttony is not self-improvement—though that will come—but love of the neighbor.

## V

I turn, therefore, to the prophetic dimension of the problem of gluttony. Our full tables are in the midst of empty tables. We should pray *"Forgive* us this day our daily bread" when our bread is never shared. The pain of overeating is qualitatively different from the pain of hunger. We complain, "I can't believe I ate the whole thing" and sing "plop, plop, fizz, fizz, oh, what a relief it is," while others have little to eat and less to sing about. So the prophetic cry of the Bible is that gluttony robs food from the plates of the poor. As Amos said: "Woe to those who . . . eat lambs from the flock, and calves from the midst of the stall . . . but are not grieved over the ruin of Joseph" (6:4-6). So God's call to you is to share from your abundance with others.

It is not a call to a sad-faced asceticism that despises all celebration. Jesus loved feasts. He said the kingdom of God is like a feast! But He also said, there is a time to feast and a time to fast. He said that our lives consist of more than what we shall eat and drink.

The time of fasting is not for some cause of self-improvement. The fast is for the sake of the neighbor. Isaiah conveyed this word from God: "The kind of fast I want is this: Remove the chains of oppression and the yoke of injustice . . . share your food with the hungry" (see Isa. 58:6-7).

When Orson Welles said, "Gluttony is not a private sin," he meant that the results of gluttony *show*—in pounds and inches. On another level he was right: Gluttony is a public sin because the overconsumption of some leads to the underconsumption of others. That is the prophetic dimension to the issue of gluttony.

Do not let gluttony dull your compassion for the poor. In the Middle Ages one of the descriptions of avarice was called "insensibility to mercy."[4] It applies to gluttony as well as greed: Our consumption betrays an "insensibility to mercy," an obliviousness to the needs of the neighbor.

Again what the Bible calls for is not an ascetic elimination of celebrations and feasts but a moderation of them for the sake of the neighbor. I recommend that you read the Mennonite Doris Janzen Longacre's book *More with Less Cookbook* as a guide for simplified eating. In it she says: ". . . the fact that in

North America we tend to feast *non-stop* can dull our festive joy.[3] When every meal tries to be a Thanksgiving dinner, what special joy does Thanksgiving Day bring? A simplification of our daily diet can make our celebration even more joyous.

## VI

Just one more word. Gluttony not only disrupts your relationship to body-self and to neighbor, it also dulls your relationship to God. That is why fasting has been an important discipline in Jewish-Christian spirituality. Staying continually full can dull our hunger not only for food but also for God. So prayer and fasting have been called for when great spiritual search is on.

But maybe that puts the cart before the horse. Maybe our overeating itself betrays a deeper, secret yearning for God. Frederick Buechner defines gluttony this way: "A glutton is one who raids the icebox for a cure for spiritual malnutrition."[9] We stuff ourselves in the vain hope that it will fill an emptiness that no bread on earth can fill.

In Dante's *Purgatory,* the gluttons are pictured praying: "O, Lord, open thou my lips and my mouth shall show forth thy praise!" Do you get Dante's point? Mouths are made for more than eating—they are made to praise God. And the hunger we feel when we fill our mouths may be a hunger only God Himself can satisfy.

That was the dynamic at play in the Gospel of John when the disciples came and said, "Rabbi, eat," and he replied, "I have food to eat of which you do not know" (John 6:31-32). Then the thickheaded disciples said something like, "Somebody must have already slipped him some lunch." But Jesus replied that they misunderstood: "My food is to do the will of him who sent me, and to accomplish his work" (v. 34).

Perhaps our greatest hunger in life is not for food but for God, not for bread you can buy in a store, but for the bread of life which has come from heaven. Such is the gift of the Christ who has come into the world. Jesus said: "I am the bread of life;

he who comes to me shall not hunger, and he who believes in me shall never thirst" (John 6:35). Eating and drinking is more than a necessity of existence, it supplies a psychic satisfaction that we are cared for and loved (and has ever since the mother's breast); and it provides a companionable experience around the table with "friends who are family and family who are friends" (to use the wonderful phrase of Grady Nutt). To these ends God is the gracious provider and cheerleader of our joy.

Gluttony is the sin which distorts this joy, making eating life's preoccupation, distorting our relationship to God, body-self, and neighbor. It is a terrible emptiness inside that tempts us toward Gluttony. Only God can satisfy that kind of hunger.

### Notes

1. Wendy Wasserstein, "Giving Into Gluttony," *Esquire* (July 1986), p. 60.
2. Cited by Fairlie, p. 159.
3. Sayers, p. 71.
4. Quoted in May, p. 60.
5. Longacre, Doris Janzen, *More with Less Cookbook* (Scottdale, Penn.: Herald Press, 1976), p. 25.
6. Buechner, p. 31.

everyone who drinks this water will be thirsty again

BUT WHOSOEVER DRINKS THE WATER THAT I SHALL GIVE HIM WILL NEVER BE THIRSTY AGAIN. THE WATER THAT I SHALL GIVE HIM WILL BE AN INNER SPRING OF A MAN WHO IS DYING OF THIRST. THE WATER THAT I SHALL GIVE HIM WILL BE AN INNER SPRING WELLING UP FOR ETERNAL LIFE.

# 8
# Lust

According to the weekly soap opera review in *The Courier-Journal*, 11-13-82, here is what happened on one of America's favorite soap operas the preceding week:

> Angry at Susan for continual drinking and lack of care for Jason, Allen decides he wants custody of his son—an idea that Monica abhors. Heather decides to move in with Scotty, but Scotty decides to move in with Susan. Lila tells Edward she knows all about his illegitimate son. After going to bed with Rose, Mark realizes that he's not over the death of his wife Katie. Claudia's parents are against her marrying Brian.

That is what is euphemistically called "Love in the Afternoon." *Love* is not the word for it. The right word is *lust* and that is the topic of this chapter.

Some of you have been anxiously awaiting this one; you may even have begun here. In one book on the seven deadly sins, the author began the chapter on lust with these words: "To the lustful among you who have turned to this chapter first!"

Lust has many faces. It is the row of middle-aged men hovering over the magazine rack catching glimpses of this month's *Playboy* or *Penthouse*, the men lined up at what Garrison Keillor calls "a sexual soup kitchen" and giving lust a bad name. "Lust is a sin," he says, "so you're supposed to be struck by it, not go to a store and shop."[1]

In America today we have created out of lust a huge store in which to come and shop—and not just the tawdry adult sex shops hawking views of women and selling bizarre selections of sexual aids. The Great American Department Store sells its wares with lust. There are few commercials left which do not use lust as the lure. Jeans commercials are more provocative today than the steamiest movies were thirty years ago. Diet drinks may appear to be magic potions for the cure of gluttony (or its results), but in fact they are sold as love potions to capture a sexy person.

Lust is in. We sell with it and shop for it. It is the ambience in a singles bar; it is the hidden agenda of a business lunch; it is the leering (not to mention avaricious) eye of the camera shooting pornography; it is the desperate look of obsessive love.

Lust is the last of the seven deadly sins, last but not least, surely not least in our hypersexualized society. But sexual openness has not brought us sexual healing. We have moved from a repressive Victorian society to an obsessive American society. In our age of "liberation," lust has been made into a virtue and women are schooled that they are entitled to as much lustfulness as men. Ah, sweet consciousness raising.

Lust is, however, a deadly sin because while it uses sexuality it does not satisfy us sexually. It has an itch that sex alone cannot scratch. It is, to use Beuchner's words, "The craving for salt of a man who is dying of thirst."[2] To be sure lust begins in an early payoff of pleasure, but soon it begins to issue into a disruption of relationships and even a numbing to pleasure itself.

# I

The subject of lust is properly a tender one. Human sexuality is an intimate domain that should stay intimate. Also, there is an extraordinary amount of unhealing among us in regard to our bodies and our sexuality. And, it is full of ambiguity: Human sexuality offers at the same time a tremendous capacity for joy and a terrible capacity for destructiveness. Also, it often seems so out of control, so unyielding to the best efforts of mind and will. It reminds us of the tenacity of original sin. A Faulkner character once described original sin this way: "Well, it's like this. I ain't got to, but I can't help it."

So we proceed tenderly.

There is a reason I have left lust until last. Too often the church has acted as if lust were the only sin. When most people say "immoral," they refer to sexual immorality. You can be prideful, slothful, envious, angry, greedy, and gluttonous and still be a respectable Christian, but woe unto you if you commit sexual sin. Dorothy Sayers entitled her essay on the seven deadly sins, "The Other Six Deadly Sins," after a young man came and said to her, "I did not know there were seven deadly sins: Please tell me the names of the other six."[3]

Theologians have handled lust with kid gloves or not at all. When John Cassian wrote his *Institutes* in the fifth century he included lust in his treatment of the deadly sins. But when I turned to its section in *The Nicene and Post Nicene Fathers,* I was confronted with a blank space. There underneath the heading of book VI entitled "On the Spirit of Fornication" were the discreet words of the editors: "We have thought best to omit altogether the translation of this book."[4] "Fools rush in where angels (and editors) fear to tread." So I proceed.

## II

Lust is the only one of the seven Deadly sins publicly confessed by a President of the United States—and in *Playboy* no less! (Lust is, however, far from the first to be committed by a President—pride, envy, anger, and greed always lurk at the White House door and Senate chambers.) Jimmy Carter confessed that he had lusted in his heart. He referred to Jesus' words in Matthew: "You have heard that it was said, You shall not commit adultery. But I say to you that every one who looks at a woman lustfully has already committed adultery with her in his heart" (5:27-28).

Carter interpreted this passage to mean that Jesus knows we all have lusts, understands them and forgives us our lusts;

therefore none of us should feel unduly judged by God nor should we be judgmental toward others. Carter correctly captured the grace of the gospel in the passage—it was meant as a rebuke to the smugness of the Pharisees who pretended to be themselves free from lust, since they had committed no act of adultery. But Jesus knew how deadly the inner preoccupation with lust could be, so there is also the demand of the gospel in this passage. Jesus was saying, "Do not lust; lust is a deadly sin."

How are we to interpret this passage? Oral Roberts said once in reference to it, that there is a difference between admiring a good-looking person and desiring that person, a distinction which most mere mortals find difficult to maintain. Isn't there some desiring in all admiring?

I would interpret the passage this way. There is no sin in the admiring/desiring of another person. Those feelings are a natural part of being human. The sin of lust is the morbid preoccupied dwelling upon this desire, which may or may not end up in an act of lust but which distorts healthy relationships with others and threatens the vows of fidelity which a married person may have made. Jesus was saying that a sin can be deadly whether or not it becomes an action like adultery. He was not condemning every person with a sexual thought as guilty of lust.

### III

What is the deadly sin of lust? Certainly as previously suggested, it is not the innocent rush of sexual excitement. To call that sin would be cruel; our calling that a sin has led to sexual repression and its child, sexual obsession.

Lust is the preoccupied and preoccupying dwelling upon objects of sexual desire. Lust is the obsessive search for sexual satisfaction which derives from a thirst no sexual expression can quench. Lust is the sexual expression (or acting out)_ of deeper needs. For example, lust can be the sexual expression of pride as a person seeks sexual conquests to bolster his or her ego. A man passing forty seeks the physical corroboration of his worth in the arms of another woman. More than lust is at work. Lust may be the expression of sloth, the compulsive search for something to fill an emptiness, to lift a despondency. Oh to lose oneself in love! Dorothy Sayers and C. S. Lewis both contended that we are most vulnerable to lust in times of despondency.

In Lewis's *The Screwtape Letters,* Screwtape, a big-wheel devil in Satan's lower-archy gives this advice to Wormwood, his young nephew, a devil who has been assigned to corrupt a person on earth:

> MY DEAR WORMWOOD,
>
> . . . I have always found that the Trough (dull, dry, depressed) periods of human undulation provide excellent opportunity for all sensual temptations, particularly those of sex. This may surprise you, because, of course, there is more physical energy, and therefore more potential appetite, at the peak periods; but you must remember that the powers of resistance are then also at their highest. . . . The attack has a much better chance of success when the man's whole inner world is drab and cold and empty.[5]

One man confessed that his sexual adventures were really a distraction, keeping his mind off the fact that his career was in shambles. Another man's lust is stirred by anxieties over loss of virility. A young woman seeks sex as a way of satisfying deeper needs for intimacy. "Looking for Mr. Goodbar," she hops from bar to bed. In all cases there is a law of diminishing returns. As Screwtape counsels his nephew: "An ever increasing craving for an ever diminishing pleasure is the formula."[6]

## IV

Lust has many faces. I mention just three; promiscuity, pornography, and adultery.

Promiscuity is casual sex. Promiscuity is the modern equivalent of what is translated in the Bible as "fornication" from the Greek word *porneia* (as in pornography). The sexual revolution has promised us sexual liberation but what we have been given instead is a new bondage: the tyranny of having to say yes. The sexual revolution has not brought us to a new Garden of Eden but rather led us from one desert to another.

In a *Village Voice* article in the early 1970s Karen Durbin called herself a "casualty of the sex war." She reported that the sexual revolution had succeeded in turning people into things. What we have today, she said, "is not love or affection or even simple friendship."

Dr. Helen Kaplan, a leading sex therapist, looks with alarm at our present trends. Guilt-ridden sex has been replaced by compulsive sex. We have to say yes. She says, "True sexual freedom is the ability to say 'no' or 'that's enough' without anxiety about it."

Are you strong enough or free enough to say no? Christ has set us free. We can say no. We have been *redeemed,* a word that means "set free from slavery." We are no longer for sale or rent. For freedom Christ has set us free. The apostle Paul said, don't give it up for a new slavery.

The biblical principle at work here is that full sexual knowing is for love's full commitment. The Hebrew word *yadah* means both "to know" and "to have sexual relations with." That primitive Hebrew insight is most important. Healthy and fulfilling sexuality is the unity of desiring and knowing. If I desire another sexually without wanting deep knowledge of the other and wanting to be in living communion with the other then I am using the other as an object.

Lust is sexual desire set apart from personal commitment. It seeks not intimate communion and deep, mutual knowing but only self-gratification. It is intrinsically lonely. It is autosexual, even when coupled with another body.

This leads to the next face of lust: pornography. A definition of pornography: The staging, filming, or photographing of actual sexual intercourse or of sexual behavior degrading to human persons for the purpose of financial profit for the makers and sexual stimulation for the viewers. It may be a symbol for lust: Sexual desire that does not seek deep personal communion but rather only self-gratification. Voyeurism is lust's way of solitary gratification. In a recent theological journal, an anonymous minister writes chillingly of his descent into hell through lust. Lust led him down the lonely path from magazines to movies to live sex shows. It was a ten-year bondage that disrupted his relationship with his wife and his God.[7]

Pornography is the path of lonely lust. By its nature it cannot satisfy. It leads its captives from one experience to another, from one perversion to another until the senses are more numbed than quenched. And we should not forget the larger social consequences of pornography: The exploitation of its "stars" and the sustaining of the illegal underground economy involving drugs, prostitution, and hard-core pornography. It will be a puzzle to future historians as to why America has tolerated such activity to the degree that we have.

The last face of lust is adultery. It is the breaking of covenant-love between spouses. Adultery is a constant temptation in America. Soap operas are a 1,001 variations on the theme of adultery. The work setting of most Americans provides more than ample opportunity. In some circles of wisdom it is not only not considered a sin, but is called a virtue, the proof of healthy marriages and a help for troubled ones. So argued Nena and George O'Neill, their *Open Marriage*,[8] so fashionable in the 1970s, reaping a whirlwind in the 1980s.

Adultery is an everpresent temptation for married persons— and even more so today. To be sure marriage does not solve lust! The apostle Paul advised the Corinthians that it was better to marry than to burn—which is the best evidence we can find that he was never married. Marriage and burning are not mutually exclusive. Adultery is one of lust's temptations, and as Jesus reminded us, it begins inwardly as a lust of the heart. Be careful when innocent attraction turns into a brooding and calculating desire for adultery.

The biblical ethic of sexuality has maintained the ideal unity of sex, love, and marriage. Healthy and satisfying sex is most possible in the context of love; love is most possible in the context of marriage; marriage is hardly possible apart from the creative and procreative communion of sex. Often we think, romantically, that love is necessary for marriage. We need to think the reverse: Marriage is necessary for love. Love is so fleeting an emotion as to be undependable; it is so powerful an emotion as to be destructive of human relationships. So we need the structure of the lifelong covenant of marriage to help us grow a deep and true love.[9] The security of such covenanting also provides a structure of relating to other persons with more freedom to be affectionate and to enjoy their company, because we know we are neither the hunter, huntress, nor hunted.

## V

These are some of the dynamics of lust. What does the Christian faith have to offer persons who wish to be free from it?

First of all it offers a proper theology of the body. As in the last chapter, I offer to you Paul's theology. The Corinthians had many of the same problems as Americans. There were some who idolized the body. Its impulses were there to be obeyed. "Go with the Flow" was the slogan. There were others who said that what you did with the body was of no concern to God; so, do with it as you please. There were those who despised the body—it was of the devil—so they sought to deny all its needs. So some of these were practicing celibate marriages. Corinth was the California of the ancient world! There were free-sex fanatics and no-sex fanatics. They believed every idea was created equal and any wild idea could be the beginning of a new religion.

Paul offered a proper biblical theology of the body: The body is not divine to be worshiped; it is not demonic to be despised; it is the temple of God's Holy Spirit, God's good gift to you, to be used for the glory of God. So glorify God in your bodies (see 1 Cor. 6:19-20).

This theology avoids a gnostic or Victorian despising of the body which can lead to dangerous repression and then to resulting obsessions. It also avoids a hedonistic acting out of every impulse which says yes to everything. We should not feel guilty over the rush of sexual excitement or the natural attraction we feel toward others—without it the race would soon be extinct, without it God's world would be far less good. But neither should we indiscriminately indulge these feelings. Repressed lust may lead to obsessive sex, but indulged lust leads to compulsive sex. A biblical theology of the body avoids both.

How do we glorify God in our bodies? We use them in service of love and love demands certain principles which direct our behavior. Christians should be the most healthy persons in regard to sexuality. We are taught the goodness of sexuality, and also the proper limits of its expression.

Some of you may be indulging your bodies in such a way that it is causing hurt in relationships. Others of you may be despising your bodies which is causing its own havoc in you. So a proper theology of the body is one help the faith gives you.

## VI

But good theology is not enough. We need grace. Grace comes first in forgiveness, a forgiveness deeper than any sin. You first need to hear: "Jesus forgives sexual mistakes." Jesus forgives you your lust. That needs to be heard loud and clear because the church has been more unforgiving on this one than any other. In remarkable contradistinction, the New Testament Gospels record a special quality of compassion Jesus had for those who had become trapped in sexual sins. Witness the woman at the well (John 4), the woman caught in adultery (John 8), or the prostitute who wet His feet with her tears and anointed Him with expensive perfume (Luke 7:36-50). Even Mary Magdalene in Jesus' closest circle of followers is thought to have been a prostitute. To each He offered the grace of forgiveness. "Your sins are forgiven; go and sin no more."

Why did He show such tender mercy to these? Perhaps because the religious folk of His day also condemned these kinds of sins so harshly. Perhaps because persons trapped in sexual sin are trying so hard to love and be loved. Lust is especially poignant; it is the distortion of the highest good and purpose of life: love. It is so close to love and yet even in its closeness so painfully far away. It is one of the "warmhearted sins," the tragic turning of an open, generous, loving heart into a way that leads to destruction. We all make mistakes at love.

So hear the tender word of pardon. Your sins are forgiven. You can be healed to the deepest level of who you are. Sexual compulsion may come from way back and way deep. God's grace can go all the way back and all the way down to offer you forgiveness, acceptance, cleansing, and healing.

And the pardon never stops. Every day we are in need of pardon, every day Christ is there to offer it. This sin, as all seven, is always nearby as temptation, no matter how far we come; so pardon is ever a welcome gift.

But grace is more than pardon. It is also power. Lust is the craving for salt of one who is dying of thirst, but Jesus offers you what He offered the woman at the well: A living water that will flow forever into our lives to quench our thirst, a water that will become a "spring of water welling up to eternal life" (John 4:14).

That living water is grace's power to break free from the bondage of lust. It curbs its compulsion. It is the Spirit's gift of self-control to help you take the practical steps necessary to guard yourself from lust's grip. It is there to pull us back on course when we slip.

That living water finally is a love that transforms all you are and all you do and all you feel into creative service of His love. Grace's power marshals all our body's energies into the highest forms of Love.

Jesus says to you, as He said to those of His day, worried and trapped by lust: I do not condemn you. You are forgiven. Come drink from my well. Here is living water that will quench your thirst now and every day. Here, I offer you a new way of love, this one not feverish or compulsive or seductive, but a love that is free and constant and true.

So go now, your head held high, your heart set free. Go and sin no more.

## Notes

1. "Lust on Wheels" *Esquire,* p. 61.

2. Buechner, p. 54.

3. Sayers, p. 63.

4. *The Nicene and Post-Nicene Fathers* (Grand Rapids: William B. Eerdmans Publishing Company, 1955), second series, vol. XI, p. 248.

5. C. S. Lewis, *The Screwtape Letters* (New York: The Macmillan Company, 1960), p. 48.

6. Ibid., p. 49.

7. *Leadership,* Fall, 1982, pp. 31-48.

8. Nena and George O'Neill, *Open Marriage* (New York: Avon Press, 1972).

9. I am indebted to Stanley Hauerwas for his essay "Sex in Public" in *A Community of Churches* (Notre Dame: University of Notre Dame Press, 1981), pp. 175-195.

# 9
# Whatever Became of Virtue?

If the word *sin* has disappeared from our modern vocabulary, *virtue* has beat an even hastier retreat. Virtue has been associated with moral priggishness—more manners than morals. We group the word with such unflattering phrases as "Victorian bluenoses" or "Puritan self-righteousness."

Who wants to be good anymore? Fulfilled? Yes. Self-actualized or successful or accomplished? Certainly! But good? Absolutely not! The question, Why be good? has a quaint sound to it; we smile at the question, and there is no longer a self-evident answer.

Some people question whether goodness is really *good*. The little girl's prayer says it all: "Dear God, make all the bad people good and all the good people nice." We've known plenty of people who paraded as good people who weren't very nice. They are what Jesus called hypocrites—play actors at goodness —or what Mark Twain called a good man in the worst sense of the word. Consequently, some people question whether goodness is really good. Someone can do virtuous acts without being a virtuous person, just as a mediocre golfer can every once in a while hit a good shot. What we would want from virtue is the ability to be consistently virtuous, as a good golfer consistently hits good shots.

Other people question whether goodness is *real*. Ours is an age of moral cynicism. Moral cynics say that there is no good or evil, only the push and pull of power. What we call virtue is only another of those things used by people to manipulate others. Ours is also a time of moral relativism. Relativists say that there is no absolute good or evil, only what is effective or not—pragmatism. Or, there is only what is healthy or not—psychologism, the replacement of moral categories with psychological ones. As I quoted Robert Coles, Harvard professor of psychiatry, earlier in his charge to the educational establishment, "replacing moral philosophy with psychology has been a disaster." Similarly, Phillip Rieff in *The Triumph of the Therapeutic* has argued that the category of truth has been replaced by the category of "psychological effectiveness."

There are others who would acknowledge that goodness is good and is real; however, they do not believe it is *possible*. They despair of goodness. They would like to be good only we do not feel we can. They have seen the dark side of human personhood in ourselves and others, and we question our motives. They have tried too many times to change, in vain; they have broken too many New Year's resolutions. Their question is not so much "Why be good?" as "How be good?"

The conviction of this book, however, is that goodness *is* good, *is* real, and *is* possible. The rest of this chapter will be devoted to three questions: What is good? (or what is virtue?), Why be good? and How be good?

## What Is Virtue?

In its original meaning in the Greek language the word for virtue, *arete*, meant power, the power to do what it is created to do. So the virtue of an eye is in its seeing, the virtue of a knife is in its ability to cut. In Homeric poems *arete* is used to describe an excellence of any kind; a fast runner displays the *arete* of his feet. So virtue is both power and excellence. Thomas Aquinas defined virtue as "a certain perfection of power,"[1] which draws on both meanings, power and the enhancement of power we call excellence. You can imagine then a virtue of the mind, or intellectual virtue, as exemplified in a scientist like Einstein or a virtue of the body as exemplified in an Olympian athlete like Mary Lou Retton.

The kind of virtue we are concerned with here is moral virtue. Moral virtue is an excellence of character which helps us fulfill our function as human persons. The good news is that moral virtue can be attained by any person anywhere, anytime. Indeed, Mortimer Adler, perhaps the leading moral philosopher in America today, says: "The only personal perfection that would appear not to depend upon any external circumstance is moral virtue."[2] Perfection of mind or body depends upon a set of opportune natural gifts and external circumstances. Moral virtue is a possibility for us all regardless of mental[3] or physical endowments and regardless of circumstances. A person of modest mental abilities can be a good person, as can a person who grows up in an immoral environment. As Sir Thomas More put it: "The times are never so bad but that a good man can live in them."

If moral virtue is the excellence of character which helps us fulfill our function as human persons, what is this function and what are some of these virtues? Our purpose as human persons is to live in communion with God and with those closest of neighbors and to reside in a just and free community with the larger family of persons. The list of virtues could be endless, but all virtues help us achieve the basic purpose. Both the Bible and the moral tradition of Western civilization have numerous lists of virtues. For the purposes of this book, I have chosen the seven virtues adapted from classical Greek culture and biblical religion, and considered to be the cream of the crop: wisdom, courage, justice, temperance, faith, hope, and love.

The seven contribute to the building of personal character and to the building up of the social fabric. Neither individuals nor society could live well without them. God has given them to us for the perfection of our character and the enhancement of our communities. Old Testament prophets saw the connection between righteousness and the health of the nation while

Plato rightly depicted the role of the four classical virtues: wisdom, justice, courage, and temperance, in the building of *The Republic.*

The virtues are at once gifts from God and habits we human folk form, habits which as they become second nature perfect the nature we were given by God at creation. Again, virtue is power (gift) and excellence (habit). More about this later.

## Why Be Good?

At one time the question "Why be good?" would have been rhetorical with a self-evident answer. No more. My own answer is this: We should be good because we were created to be good. Goodness is how we fulfill our purpose. When Jesus said "Be ye perfect," He meant: Fulfill the purpose for which you were created.

When we fulfill our purpose, we are "happy." It was not accident that both biblical religion and Greek philosophy recognized the connection between goodness and happiness. The Greek philosophers said that the end of life was happiness, *eudaimonia,* and that a prerequisite for this good life was the exercise of moral virtue.

Mortimer Adler, the contemporary representative of this moral tradition, says that happiness is not the psychological feeling of happiness which comes when our desires are met, but rather is the ethical happiness of "a complete life well lived."[4] Such happiness depends upon the exercise of moral virtue. But that in itself is not enough; agreeing with Aristotle, Adler argues that in addition to a life lived in accordance with virtue, there must also be the presence of other good things, such as health, freedom, and a moderate degree of prosperity. Then a person can be truly happy.

The biblical tradition would not compute into the equation of happiness the necessity of health, wealth, and freedom, though these surely help us to be happy. Saint Augustine modified the Greek notion of happiness when in a tract called *The Happy Life* he said: "Happy is the man who in the course of a complete life, attains everything he desires, provided he desire nothing amiss."[5] The proviso is important.

The biblical notion of happiness goes beyond the Greek notion by introducing the pleasure God takes in us and we take in God and in ourselves when we follow the way of righteousness and virtue. In the movie *Chariots of Fire,* Eric Liddel, a young Scottish missionary, is planning to go to a China mission, but first he is seeking to "glorify God in his body" by winning an Olympic gold medal. Eric's sister is trying to persuade him to stop his running and return immediately to mission work. He replies: "I believe God made me for a purpose: That's China. But he also made me fast, and when I run I feel His pleasure." When we train ourselves in moral virtue, we feel His pleasure. It is the perfection of our created nature. When we delight in God and in His righteousness, we experience God's delight in us. As Psalm 147 expresses it: "The Lord takes pleasure in those who fear him, in those who hope in his steadfast love" (v. 11).

The happiness of which I write is deeper than psychological happiness or feeling happy. It is the deep satisfaction we experience when we know we are doing what God created us to do and when we are the kind of person He created us to be.

We were made for goodness. In His own image God created us, male and female, and when He made us He looked at us and called us *good* (Gen. 1:26-31). The New Testament sings forth that the image in which we were made is the image of the Christ: 'He is the image of the invisible God, and we were created "in him, . . . through him and for him" (Col. 1:15). Christ is the truest truth about who we are. The image of God in us is the capacity to love and be loved, to live in communion with God and in community with others.[6] The apostle Paul explains that we are saved by grace through faith (which means when we receive it as the gift it is) and not by good works. He then adds: "For we are his workmanship [his *poiema,* in the Greek, we might translate, his poem or his work of art] created in Christ Jesus for good works, which God prepared beforehand, that we should walk in them" (Eph. 2:10). Among those good works that God prepared for us that we should walk in them are virtues like wisdom, courage, justice, temperance, faith, hope, and love. These virtues and the deeds which issue from them show us becoming "the work of art" God made us to be.

We were created in God's image to be good. When we are not good, we become strangers to ourselves and to our Creator. Saint Augustine prayed in his *Confessions:* "You were right before me; but I had moved away from myself. I could not find myself; how much less, then, could I find you?"[7]

Why be good? Because we were created to be good, because therein do we fulfill our created purpose as persons, because in being good we experience God's deep pleasure in us and our pleasure in God and in ourselves.

Goodness is no guarantee for success. Virtue will help you succeed and help you be happy, healthy, and free, but it is no guarantee. The Bible teaches us that the way of righteousness leads to life and success, and that of wickedness leads to death and destruction; however, it is not always, automatically, or quickly so. Bad things happen to good people and good things happen to bad people. The Bible speaks realistically about the good who suffer and the wicked who prosper. So goodness is no guarantee for success; indeed the quintessential good man, Jesus of Nazareth, was executed on a Roman cross.

The deeper happiness than the Greek notion of *eudaimonia* is Jesus' notion on *blessedness.* If you read Jesus' Beatitudes (Matt. 5:3-12; Luke 6:21-23) you see the picture of a deep happinessblessedness which is life lived in the joy of God's presence and in loving community with God's children. There are few external reasons for happiness depicted in the Beatitudes, but life therein is marked by happiness and fulfillment.

Why be good? We are good because our goodness is the gift of our communion with God who is ground of our being and because our goodness is the foundation of our communion with God, neighbor, and self.

## How Be Good?

This question, "How be good?" may be the one you have been waiting for. The answer is twofold and is inherent in the very word *virtue*. In its root meanings virtue means power and excellence. That is, it is both gift and habit. In the ancient use of the word an Olympic runner like Eric Liddel would have been said to have the virtue of being fast and the virtue of discipline, which made him not only fast but also excellent.

So moral virtue is the power of goodness (a gift from God) and it is the habit of goodness (our own moral training and discipline).

Virtue is a natural endowment perfected by habit; it is a habit which has become almost as sure as instinct. As stated before, when virtue becomes our second nature it is the perfection of our created nature. In his novel, *A Single Pebble*, John Hersey describes his experience observing a man rescuing a boy from death:

> It was the head tracker's marvellous swift response that captured my admiration at first, his split-second solicitiousness when he heard a cry of pain, his finding in mid-air, as it were, the only way to save the injured boy. But there was more to it than that. His action, which could not have been mulled over in his mind, showed a deep instinctive love of life, a compassion, an optimism, which made me feel very good.[8]

What a marvelous description of virtue: "A deep instinctive love of life, a compassion, an optimism, which made me feel very good." The truly good people I have known, people of true virtue, have been like that, and they have made me feel very good.

This kind of goodness is a gift from the Creator, an evidence of natural grace, and it is also a habit, a discipline consisting of difficult choices and the day-by-day, step-by-step determination to do what is good. As a gift it must be received; as a habit it must be exercised. Which leads to two questions: Where do we receive it? and How do we decide to be a moral person?

Where do we receive the gift of virtue? I reiterate that the capacity for virtue is a gift of creation; in nascent form it is a natural endowment given everyone. But that is not enough. Virtue must also be nurtured in intentional communities which cherish virtue: the home, the school, and the church or synagogue. These basic institutions have as their vocation the teaching and living of the moral life. Moral virtue cannot be truly taught unless it is a lived reality in community.

There has been spirited debate for thousands of years as to whether virtue can be taught. The Bible assumes it can be:

> Israel, remember this! The Lord—and the Lord alone—is our God. Love the Lord your God with all your heart, with all your soul, and with all your strength. Never forget these commands that I am giving you today. Teach them to your children. Repeat them when you are at home and when you are away, when you are resting and when you are working. Tie them on your arms and wear them on your foreheads as a reminder. Write them on the doorpost of your houses and on your gates (Deut. 6:4-9, GNB).

Socrates and Aristophanes argued whether the family or schoolmaster was the best teacher of virtue.[9] Socrates argued that moral virtue cannot be taught in the way we teach mathematics or music. The freedom of our wills and our unpredictable, uncontrollable passions make the transfer of virtue from teacher to student much more precarious than, say, the transfer of mathematical knowledge. And as for the role of the family or religious community in the transfer of virtue, Jesus said that we are children of Abraham not by benefit of bloodliness or even participation in religious services but only as we do the will of God. We can be from "good stock" and be very "religious" and still be morally bankrupt.

We sadly concur. Virtuous parents work diligently to raise their children to be persons of moral virtue, but one turns out to be a good person while another forsakes morality. And the converse is true: Some people survive morally twisted homes and become persons of virtue. What are the necessary ingredients, then, in becoming a person of moral virtue?

**Ingredient One: The Creator's Gift.** As said previously,

God gives to every person the capacity for moral goodness. We are basically good. Our conscience can be ill-formed or get out of whack and fail us like a bad thermometer which can no longer pick up a temperature, but God gives us all the capacity for goodness.

*Ingredient Two: The Community's Instruction.* We need the morally intentional communities of family, church/synagogue, and school. Philosophers may debate whether virtue can be taught or how best it is taught, but we affirm the necessity of the community's instruction. We are social beings shaped by our communities.

But while these first two ingredients are necessary to a person's becoming a person of virtue, they are not sufficient. For while all people are given the gift of virtue by God and while many are taught virtue, far fewer actually become virtuous persons. And other people rise above the moral level of their community. Something else is needed.

That something else is *Ingredient Three: Conversion.* Conversion is the experience of the person who wakes up to the importance of being a moral person. The Bible speaks of "the enlightening of the eyes of the heart," of "scales falling from the eyes," of "coming to oneself," of a turnabout or a waking up, of hearts being softened and darkened minds finally seeing the light. Such is the language of conversion. The images speak to a new way of seeing, feeling, thinking, and behaving.

Such conversion may come slowly, like the slow dawning of a summer day, or it may come upon us like a flash of lightning. It may evolve over years of exposure or, precipitated by a life crisis, it may instantly change everything.

However, whenever it comes, our eyes are opened and we determine to be persons of moral integrity. We receive and exercise the gift of virtue. We will never be perfect, but now we see what we want to be and how important it is, and we seek God's help in being the best, responsible, and whole person we can be. Ingredient One, Creator's Gift, Ingredient Two, Com-

munity's Instruction, and Ingredient Three, Conversion lead to
becoming a person of moral virtue.

### Some Last Suggestions

What I have said may still not be concrete enough to answer
how Be good. So here are some first steps.

*You need to want to be good.* You need what the great
British preacher James Reid called "moral sincerity." I am
sure that if with all your heart you want to be good, God will
not withhold the power of goodness. So the beginning is the
prayer, "O God, give me the heart to want to be good."

For a small number of people there may be some deep dynamic, psychological issues which keep them from either wanting to be good or being able to be good. If prayer, worship, the
nurture of your religious community, and your own diligent
efforts do not work, you may well choose to seek the help of a
professional therapist or counselor.

*You need to start where you are.* Ask for God's forgiveness
for past sins and receive it. God does not want you languishing
in guilt or remorse over the past. God's forgiveness helps you
take the first giant step toward spiritual freedom and moral
excellence.

Once you take the first step, you will be glad to be on your
path toward goodness. There really is no other way to fulfillment, and no halfhearted attempt will do. As P. T. Geach put
it: ". . . nobody can safely settle for a mediocre degree of virtue."[11]

*Seek Christ and the power of His grace within.* His power
of love will stir in you new capacities for moral virtue.

*Become an active participant in some morally serious
community such as a church* where you can get communal
reinforcement and guidance for your journey.

*Make a determination not to do anything you know is
wrong.* To invite the inner conflict of doing something you
know is wrong at a point where you are trying to grow in virtue
is self-defeating. A priest once went to Mother Teresa and

asked how to live out his vocation as a priest. She replied: "Spend one hour a day in adoration of your Lord and never do anything you know is wrong and you will be all right." That is good advice for any of us.

***Read this book (!) and other books which encourage the moral life.*** Your mental input makes a difference. As the apostle Paul said: "Whatever is true, whatever is honorable, whatever is just, whatever is pure, whatever is lovely, whatever is gracious, if there is any excellence [*arete,* virtue], if there is anything worthy of praise, think about these things" (Phil. 4:8).

## Notes

1. Summa Theologica I-II,55,1, trans. Fathers of the English Dominican Province (Chicago: Encyclopaedia Britannica, 1952), as cited in Stanley Hauerwas, *A Community of Character* (Notre Dame: University of Notre Dame Press, 1981), p. 111.

2. Mortimer J. Adler, *A Vision of the Future* (New York: Macmillan Publishing Company, 1984), p. 89.

3. Lawrence Kohlberg, drawing upon Piaget's theory of cognitive development, has conceptualized a stage process of moral development which depends on cognitive and social development. I essentially agree with his work; where I would make a point of emphasis is that a person can be a genuinely good person at any of these stages if cognitive incapacity makes progress to a higher stage impossible.

See Lawrence Kohlberg, "Stages of Moral Development as a Basis for Moral Education" in *Moral Education,* C. M. Beck, B. S. Guttenden, E. V. Sullivan (Great Britain: University of Toronto Press, 1971), pp. 23-92.

4. Adler, pp. 115-116.

5. Adler, pp. 91-92.

6. See Daniel Day Williams, *The Spirit and the Forms of Love* (New York: Harper & Row Publishers, 1968), pp. 130 ff.

7. Augustine, *Confessions,* V,II,2.

8. Cited in Phillipa Foot, *Virtues and Vices* (Oxford: Basil Blackwell, 1978), p. 4.

9. Russell Kirk, "Virtue: Can It Be Taught?" *Modern Age* (Summer/Fall, 1982, pp. 343-349).

10. Adler, pp. 107 ff.

11. P. T. Geach, *The Virtues* (Cambridge: Cambridge University Press, 1977), p. 149.

THE FEAR
OF THE
LORD
IS
THE
BEGINNING
OF
WISDOM

# 10
# Wisdom

You have just traveled through the land of the seven deadly sins. I hope you enjoyed the journey and have learned better how to escape their clutches. In our world there is enough attention given to the tawdry and immoral. Why not take a look at what is morally excellent? I called the seven deadly sins "obstacles to grace" because they block the gracious activity of God in our lives; the virtues I call "evidence of grace" because these virtues are evidence of the goodness and grace of God within us.

The mystery of evil seems to capture our mind's attention. Why not give equal time to the mystery of goodness? The virtues speak to the mystery of goodness, the power of righteousness, the evidence of grace. First, wisdom.

## I

In the *Wizard of Oz,* Dorothy meets a scarecrow who is in search of a brain. So is the world in search of wisdom. Wisdom, first of all, is the search for truth. To use a distinction the Greek philosophers made, it is the intellectual virtue of knowing the truth. Our civilization depends upon truth for its very survival. There are two enemies of truth in our world today. The first is ignorance—not knowing the truth. For some, ignorance is their plight, for others it is their badge. The South, for example, has always had a perverse pride in its anti-intellectualism. The second enemy of truth is ideology. Ideology is the twisting of truth for the purposes of power; propaganda is in its voice. Nazism and Communism are the two most dramatic forms of ideology in our century, but we are all vulnerable to its lure.

Christians should never be timid in their search for truth, any truth, all truth, wherever it may be found. God is the author of all reality so all truth is finally one and all truth leads to God.

The Book of Proverbs pictures wisdom as the beloved daughter of God begat at creation. Hear her voice:

> The Lord created me at the beginning of his work,
>    the first of his acts of old. . . .
> When he marked out the foundations of the earth,
>    then I was beside him, like a [little child];
> and I was daily his delight,
>    rejoicing before him always (Prov. 8:22, 29b-30).

Wisdom is the truth of the universe, established from the beginning. All sciences, in their search, engage in "the play of wisdom."[1] As children of God, Christians should not be enemies of truth, but rather truth's best friend. As we discover any truth—historical, scientific, or spiritual—we "think God's thoughts after God."

## II

But wisdom is more than the search for truth, more than an "intellectual virtue." It is also the moral virture we call prudence. Prudence has to do with practical and moral reasoning, good common sense about how to live. C. S. Lewis wrote: "Prudence means practical common sense, taking the trouble to think out what you are doing and what is likely to come of it."[2]

You see, the scarecrow, and we as well, need a brain for more than discovering what is true; we also need a brain to determine what is right. This is where prudence comes in. We can have the intellectual virtue and not be a morally virtuous person, but prudence is essential if we are to be morally virtuous.[3]

In the Old Testament, wisdom is associated with Solomon.

The Bible reports that Solomon was renowned as the wisest person on earth. He himself uttered over three thousand proverbs. His most famous display of wisdom was the time two women came with a child, both claiming to be the mother. Solomon ordered the baby cut in half. The first woman cried, "No, it is mine, but I cannot bear to have it killed. Give it to her." The second woman said, "Go ahead, if one of us can't have it, neither should." Solomon then declared the first woman the true mother and gave it to her. (See 1 Kings 4:16-27.)

The Bible is full of homey, practical wisdom. The Book of Proverbs is a prime example. Often Old Testament study emphasizes the role of prophet, priest, and king, but there were also the sages like Solomon who taught practical commonsense wisdom for daily living—the spiritual/moral counterparts to sayings like: "Don't spit in the wind" or "You can't rollerskate in a buffalo herd." Here are a couple of modern proverbs: "Never attribute to malice that which can be adequately explained by stupidity." (A good antidote for paranoia.) Or this wise saying: "We are worn down less by the mountain we must climb than the grain of sand in our shoe."

Here are some examples of Wisdom from Proverbs:

> Pride goes before destruction (16:18).
>
> He who is greedy for unjust gain makes trouble for his household,
>     but he who hates bribes will live (15:27).
>
> A cheerful heart is a good medicine,
>     but a downcast spirit dries up the bones (17:22).
>
> Wine is a mocker, strong drink a brawler;
>     and whoever is led astray by it is not wise (20:1).
>
> He who is slow to anger has great understanding,
>     but he who has a hasty temper exalts folly (14:29).
>
> He who is slack in work
>     is a brother to him who destroys (18:9).

We need the Old Testament sage along with prophet, priest, and king. We need Proverbs not just Amos, and James along with Paul. The great sage of the modern age was Samuel Johnson. One of the outstanding intellectuals of modern times, he was also a profound moral philosopher. Of his work as a moralist, he said that his purpose was "to consider the moral discipline of the mind, and to promote the increase of virtue rather than learning." As a man of learning he was without peer, having produced single-handedly the first *Dictionary of the English Language,* but he knew that knowledge without moral virtue was nothing. We survive only by the moral wisdom of the ages, so Johnson rightly said that we humans "more frequently require to be reminded than informed."[4] Wisdom is a practical reminder of how to live happily and healthily.

### III

As you enter the cathedral of Notre Dame in Paris, to the side of the front door the virtues and vices are depicted through sculpture in a double row of figures. On the top row the virtues are depicted by women holding shields with appropriate symbols. Below are the corresponding vices depicted by men engaged in the vice. For Wisdom, a woman is holding a shield with the symbol of the serpent. The serpent has been from ancient days a symbol of wisdom. Jesus Himself taught us that we were to be "wise as serpents and innocent as doves" (Matt. 10:16).

To Jesus wisdom was being smart about your spiritual health. The foolish man knows disaster is on the way but does nothing to prepare for it. So Jesus told a parable of the shrewd manager. The master fires the manager of his farm; but the manager is shrewd. He uses his last hours on the job to make friends with the tenant farmers under his supervision. He juggles the books for them so that their debts to the master are greatly reduced. Jesus surprises us by commending the manager's shrewdness or wisdom and says to us: "I wish you were as shrewd about your spiritual/moral lives as the children of darkness are about physical things" (see Luke 16:8-9). He instructed us to be as "wise as serpents" when it comes to our spiritual lives, hence the Christian symbol of wisdom as a serpent.

So one part of wisdom is not being dumb about your spiritual welfare. Jesus reasoned that if your foot has gangrene you cut it off to save your life; so with your moral life: You need to remove at whatever cost that which is killing you spiritually and morally (Matt. 5:29-30;18:7-9).

If you are a regular user of alcohol, it is likely that it has control over you and you need to be smart enough to get rid of it. If your friends are influencing you to do things you know are wrong, you need to be smart enough to change friends. Whatever unhealthy influence keeps you from being the best you can be, you need to get smart enough to keep away from it. What is wise is to fill your life with good influences, to think about what is good.

Get smart about the moral life. There are moral principles which if broken, break us. As the apostle Paul said, "Do not be deceived; God is not mocked; for whatever a man sows, that he will also reap" (Gal. 6:7).

## IV

Wisdom, ultimately, is hearing and obeying God's Word. God's Word gives us instructions for a safe journey through life. So Proverbs says: "The fear of the Lord is the beginning of wisdom" (9:10). Wisdom begins in reverence and is made manifest in obedience.

Reverence is the beginning of wisdom because wisdom begins by knowing the limits of your own wisdom. Wisdom is made manifest then in obedience because in obedience we yield our lives to a way beyond the reach of our minds to fully comprehend.

Thomas Hobbes used the metaphor of the highway lined with hedges. The King, he said, has placed hedges along the road, not to stop travelers in their journey, but to keep them in the way. If you go off the highway, hoping to take a short cut, you go at your own peril. You will have no map of the open country and in it you will meet many perils, dangerous cliffs, bogs, deserts, trackless forests, wild beasts, and robbers.[5]

God's Word supplies the hedges along the highway. The Ten Commandments, the Sermon on the Mount, the moral teaching throughout the Bible supply the hedge. If you jump the hedge and head for the open country, it is a journey without maps and a journey of many hazards.

To be sure, there are places along life's highway where the hedge is not clearly marked or where it is thin and unrecognizable. We may find ourselves suddenly in unmarked country, morally speaking. There are some moral dilemmas for which God's Word supplies no clear markings: "Thou shalt not kill" is clear, but what about when your nation is attacked, what about the young teenager pregnant by rape considering abortion, what about a loved one kept alive only on machines? However, we should see these as exceptional cases and should not use their existence as an excuse to jump over the *clearly defined* hedges along the way. The Ten Commandments are clearly marked and always right. Breaking them is always wrong.

The foolish person finds rationalizations to jump the hedge. History is littered by the destruction caused by brilliant persons who were morally foolish. All of us bear scars from those unfortunate side trips across the hedge and over into an unknown moral wilderness.

The beginning of wisdom is the fear of the Lord; the manifestation of wisdom is the obedience of faith.

Our land totters on the edge of moral chaos today because we are obliterating the hedges. We have made up loopholes in God's law. We are told that if the motive is right and the heart has love, then it doesn't matter what we do. But whose motives can be perfectly pure? And love is such a slippery word. Our hearts are infinitely self-deceptive. So we need hedges.

We are told that deeds are judged by their consequences. "The end justifies the means" we are taught—a lesson that is leading us to destruction. Who of us can calculate the consequences of our deeds? We need a moral way more sure than the determination of motive or the calculation of consequence. We need hedges. We need rules that are always right. Wisdom is knowing the necessity of hedges along the highway and the willingness to follow their guidance.

Jesus told a parable of a wise man who built his house on rock and the foolish man who built his house on sand. The storms came and destroyed the house built on sand, but the house built on rock was saved. The wise man, the one whose house is built on rock, is the one who hears and obeys God's Word. The foolish man hears but does not obey.

## Conclusion

I have called the virtues "evidence of grace." And I ask you, Can wisdom be good news? Can it be evidence of grace?

Surely the search for truth is a pathway laden with grace. We have been created to seek the truth and know the truth—and truth always sets us free. Surely that is good news.

But what about the moral wisdom which is hearing and obeying the law of God? Can the law really be good news to us? Can it really be, as the psalmist said, "Sweeter than honey, more dear than gold"? (see Ps. 19:10). For some the law only represents a harsh legalism devoid of love's spirit. It has been more a prison than the power of goodness.

But when we are wandering lost in the wasteland of moral chaos the sight of hedges can look awfully good. And Christ Himself comes to put His arms around us and lead us back to the King's highway. That is why Karl Barth could call the law of God "Law as a Form of the Gospel."

Wisdom is a natural grace God gives to all as a gift of creation. It is also a special grace given in Jesus Christ, for as the New Testament proclaims, Jesus Christ is the Wisdom of God and He comes to dwell in us.

When Christ comes to dwell in us, then the law of God is no longer commandments inscribed in stone, but commandments written on our hearts. It is more than hedges along the highway, it is the power of love within. When Christ comes to dwell, it is not only a law we *ought* to obey, it is one we *want* to obey—sometimes anyway! When Christ comes to dwell, it is not only a law we *must* obey, it is one we *can* obey.

You may be at the place in your life where you realize you have not been smart about your moral existence. The Bible offers you the way of righteousness and shows you where the hedges are and invites you to follow. Jesus Christ, God's Wisdom come in human flesh, can become God's Wisdom dwelling in you. As you invite Him in, the moral law of God becomes "sweeter than honey," your delight. His power of love becomes in you the power to be good.

### Notes

1. Samuel Terrien, *The Elusive Presence* (New York: Harper & Row, 1978), pp. 350 ff.

2. C. S. Lewis, *Mere Christianity* (New York: Macmillan Publishing Company, 1952), p. 74.

3. Mortimer Adler, *A Vision of the Future*, pp. 97-98.

4. Cited in W. Jackson Bate, *Samuel Johnson*, (New York: Harcourt, Brace, Jovenovich, 1975), p. 234.

5. Cited in P. T. Geach, *The Virtues*, pp. 88-89.

# BE OF GOOD COURAGE

AND HE SHALL STRENGTHEN YOUR HEART ALL YE THAT

## HOPE IN THE LORD

# 11
# Courage

In the Notre Dame sculpture of the virtues and vices, courage is pictured as a woman with a shield upon which is emblazoned a lion. Cowardice, just beneath, is a man running from a rabbit. In the *Wizard of Oz*, Dorothy meets a lion who is in search of his courage. Nothing seems more pathetic than a lion without courage; it is like an eagle without wings. If courage is seemly for a lion, it is also for us human persons. For courage is the inner strength to be whom God made and called us to be. Courage is perhaps the most crucial of the seven virtues because if it goes, they all go. Samuel Johnson, the great sage of the modern age, said of courage: "Unless a man has that virtue, he has no security for preserving any other."

This chapter is not only about courage but also about heroes and heroines, for there can be no hero in any arena of life unless that person has courage. Whether a hero in battle like Audie Murphy, a hero in thought like Galileo, a hero in compassion like Mother Teresa, or a hero in morality like Daniel or Sir Thomas More, courage is what is essential. Courage is the strength to hold fast to wisdom, justice, temperance, faith, hope, and love.

To study courage is to study heroes because courage is what makes heroes—and because heroes teach us courage and all the other virtues which it preserves. Over a century ago Thomas Carlyle wrote a book called *Heroes and Hero Worship*. In it he said: "We cannot look, however imperfectly, upon a great man, without gaining something by him. He is the living light-fountain, which it is good and pleasant to be near." Let us look more closely at courage now and at some of its heroic practitioners.

# I

Courage was defined by Plato as the virtue of the soldier. It was the civic virtue required to defend the city against invasion. In a day of frequent war between the city-states, that was no inconsiderable virtue. *Andreia* it was called in the Greek, literally *manliness.* The Latin word for the virtue was *fortitudo,* literally *strength.* Both words had strong military connotations.

It is interesting that the Bible's words for courage have less to do with manly strength and more to do with heart. Courage is a heart word. "Life up your hearts, be of good courage," the Scriptures say. In fact, in the New Testament the Greek word for the virtue of courage, *andreia,* is nowhere used. Instead, phrases are used that have to do with strength of heart, boldness of speech, and the endurance of faith and hope. Interestingly enough, the English, French, and German words for courage have to do with the heart. To have courage is to have heart or spirit.

At the most elemental and basic level, courage is the ability to withstand fear and the threat of pain and death. A nation will not survive unless it has citizens with such courage. This kind of courage, however, is more than a military virtue. Physical courage is needed daily. G. K. Chesterton remarked that people would often not be born but for the courage of their mothers. Courage is needed by every woman who endures the physical dangers of pregnancy and walks through the valley of the shadow of death to give birth to children. It is the virtue of fire fighters and policemen. It is the virtue of the person who dives into the water to save a drowning man.

Some may call such physical courage a "biological grace" because at a moment of crisis the body is filled with adrenalin

and the blood pulses with heroism. So we give thanks for this
natural evidence of grace. The saying goes that "courage is fear
that has said its prayers." That is true, but courage is often a
gift from God before the prayers are spoken—when fear has
silenced our voices. We should honor physical courage and
thank God for this natural evidence of grace.

## II

But courage is more than physical; it is also moral. This is the
courage we learned as we studied about Daniel and sang "Dare
to Be Brave, Dare to Be True." Bernard Haring, the great
Catholic moral theologian, says that courage ". . . gives us
strength and readiness to endure every kind of suffering, and
even death itself, for a just cause, for the Kingdom of God, or
our own eternal salvation."[1]

This reminds us of an important truth: While every virtue
needs courage in order to survive, courage needs the other
virtues in order to be true courage. It is not the virtue of courage to risk your life to murder someone, to fight for an unjust
cause, or to do something foolish. As P. T. Geach, a contemporary British moral philosopher, says, "There can be no virtue
in courage . . . if the cause for which this is done is worthless
or positively vicious."[2] It was courage for early Christians to
face the lions rather than bow to Caesar. It was not courage for
Jim Jones to drink his poisoned beverage. Aristotle made the
distinction between wisdom which knows the means to good
ends and cleverness which knows the means to all ends. Just
so, we should distinguish between courage which faces danger
for a just, wise, and good end and rashness or guts that faces
danger for any end.

Let us take Daniel as a hero. The story of Daniel is an epic
of moral courage. Taken from his home as a young teenager,
Daniel was brought to Babylon where he was trained in the
Babylonian court. There he exercised the virtue of courage by
saying no to the king's demand. The courageous Christian must
learn to say no. It is the only word that can keep you free.

Without no you are no longer your true self but only a reflection of your culture. Henry Van Dyke said of courage: "Courage is the standing army of the soul which keeps it from conquest, pillage and slavery."

Learn to say no. It will keep you free. It will save your soul. No tyranny is greater than the tyranny of having to say yes to everything.

Daniel was taken to the Babylonian court, given a Babylonian name, Belteshazzar, offered a good Babylonian education, and given the king's Babylonian diet of rich foods and wine. Daniel said yes to the name and education but said no to the diet. Note that he didn't say no to everything. If courage is the strength to say no, wisdom is the ability to know when to say yes and when to say no. To say no to everything is not moral courage, it is muleheadedness. It is not moral integrity, it is priggishness. Daniel accepted the best of Babylonian education and the Babylonian name, but he said no to the Babylonian diet. That was one part wisdom and one part courage.

He demonstrated his courage two other ways. The king summoned him to interpret a dream. When Daniel heard the dream he knew it meant bad news for the king. It was a prophecy of judgment and a call for repentance. Daniel knew that the king, as all kings, had a bad habit of treating as bad news those people who brought bad news, but he knew that unless he conveyed God's word of judgment there would be no hope of repentance and restoration; so he risked his neck and interpreted the dream honestly. It eventually saved the kingdom, for the king did come into his right mind and repent. That took courage—to speak the truth regardless of the consequences.

Then there was the final episode, when the next king, Darius, ordered that if anyone prayed publicly to any god except the king, he would be thrown to the lions. Daniel had a public pattern of prayer; he refused to alter it in order to save his life and was thrown to the lions. We know the end of the story. When the king came down the next morning to see what was left of Daniel, there he was playing with the lions like they were a litter of kittens. "An angel shut their mouths," Daniel said, but the old line is true as well: The lions couldn't eat him because he was all backbone.

Let me offer another hero—another friend of a king who found himself caught in a decision between virtue and death. Sir Thomas More—scholar, lawyer, ambassador, Lord Chancellor, and saint. England probably has not seen a more learned, pious, and courageous man. Samuel Johnson said of him, "He was the person of the greatest virtue these islands ever produced."

Henry VIII became obsessed that Thomas More publicly affirm the king's supremacy over the church and endorse his divorce of Catherine and remarriage to Ann Boleyn. Thomas More had done all he could to avoid the confrontation and had refused to publicly condemn the king. But for the king that was not enough. He ordered that Thomas More publicly take an oath. More refused to do so because it would have been a lie and his personal integrity would not allow him to lie. Robert Bolt's drama, *A Man for All Seasons*, captured the moment. His daughter begged him to take the oath saying that God would know his heart. Thomas More replied: "When a man takes an oath, Meg, he's holding his own self in his own hands. Like water. (He cups his hands) And if he opens his fingers *then*, he need't hope to find himself again."[3]

Meg, his daughter, argued that if the state were only half good, he would be lauded as great: "It's not your fault the state's three-quarters bad." More replied:

> If we lived in a State where virtue was profitable, common sense would make us good, and greed would make us saintly. And we'd live like animals or angels in the happy land that *needs* no heroes. But since in fact we see that avarice, anger, envy, pride, sloth, lust and stupidity commonly profit far beyond humility, chastity, fortitude, justice and thought, and (we) have to choose, to be human at all . . . why then perhaps we *must* stand fast a little—even at the risk of being heroes.[4]

And choose More did. He chose to die rather than to lie because to lie would be to be less than God made and called him to be. That is courage. So is courage necessary for us, if we are to be the persons God made us to be.

Another person of great courage was the black woman, Sojourner Truth. Born a slave named Isabella around 1797, she became a crusader for emancipation for the slaves and new rights for women. She was converted in a dramatic fashion when the Spirit of Jesus came to her to express His love and say to her, "I know you! I know you!" When given her freedom in New York in 1827, Isabella went to New York City where she worked cooking, cleaning, and caring for the sick. Then God gave her a new name, Sojourner Truth, and she traveled throughout the country speaking against the sin of slavery. She would preach and teach and sing.

Often clergymen challenged her right to speak to men— women were to keep silent. Once confronted by some males in the audience, she replied:

> Some say woman can't have as much rights as a man cause Christ wasn't a woman. Where did Christ come from? From God and a woman. Men had nothing to do with him. If the first woman God ever made was strong enough to turn the world upside down all alone, all women together ought to be able to turn it back and get it right side up again and now that they are asking to do it, men better let 'em.[5]

The crowd burst into applause. Sojourner Truth was a righteous force at work to end injustice. Without courage, she would never have made an impact. And the story of her courage brings to mind today's heroines—Winnie Mandela and Coretta Scott King.

### III

We may never be called to such a dramatic demonstration of courage, but we face the choices every day and every day we hold our selfhood in our hands like water and choose whether to save it by courage or to open our fingers and lose it. That is the test of moral courage. But there is another form of courage

I would like to offer to you, beyond physical courage, beyond moral courage, it is existential courage, the courage it takes to live and to die in face of pain, darkness, and sin. It is what Paul Tillich called *The Courage to Be*. In philosophical language he defined it thus: "The courage to be is the ethical act in which man affirms his own being in spite of those elements of his existence which conflict with his essential self-affirmation."[6]

We, all of us, face three threats to our self-affirmation: (1) The anxiety of death; (2) The anxiety of meaningless; and (3) the anxiety of guilt. We all have days when one or a combination of these makes us hate life or hate ourselves: The specter of our own deaths or the deaths of those we love; the darkness of meaninglessness or emptiness; the feeling of guilt and condemnation.

Courage is demanded in order to face life and choose life in spite of these threats. God's grace comes to us in the words "You are accepted." Courage is accepting God's acceptance; it is accepting our acceptance by faith. How do we do this? In *The Looking Glass*, Walter Farrell says of Jesus and Mary: "On Calvary there was one man brave enough to die and one woman brave enough to go on living, so all men (and women) may know that life and death demand the same ingredient of courage."

It takes courage to raise a family by yourself because a spouse has died or when divorce has made yours a one-parent family. It takes courage to live alone after fifty years of marriage. It takes courage to get out of bed and go on and choose life when depression has squeezed out every bit of light and every bit of hope in your being. It takes courage to go on when you see no light at the end of the tunnel. It takes courage to go on when your sin has destroyed your life, family, and reputation. It takes courage to go on when it seems the world honors no virtue and rewards evil more than the good.

The courage to be comes from Calvary, because at Calvary one man was brave enough to die and one woman brave enough to go on living. The courage to be in face of death comes from Calvary because the cross and resurrection shout: Death is not the final word, life is; hate is not the final word, love is; the grave has not the final word, God does.

The courage to be in face of meaninglessness comes from Calvary—where bad men absurdly killed the only good man—because Jesus could cry out "My God, my God, why hast thou forsaken me?" and then cry, "Father, into thy hands I commit my spirit!" At Calvary the terrible silence of the cross was endured until the trumpet sounds of Easter.

The courage to be in face of guilt and condemnation comes from Calvary because there we hear Him say about us, "Father forgive them for they know not what they do," and because we hear His apostle say to us, "There is therefore now no condemnation for those who are in Christ Jesus" (Rom. 8:1).

Courage then is an evidence of grace, the courage to live and to die in the face of death, meaninglessness, and guilt.

J. M. Barrie, author of *Peter Pan,* was giving his final rector's address for the convocation at Saint Andrews. He held up a tattered letter written to him from Captain Scott, the explorer who died exploring the South Pole. It was discovered in his clothes by those who found his body and given to Barrie. Hear Scott's words to Barrie:

> Hoping this letter may be found and sent to you. I write you a word of farewell. . . . Goodbye—I am not at all afraid of the end, but sad to miss many a simple pleasure which I had planned. . . . We are in a desperate state—feet frozen, etc., no fuel, and a long way from food, but it would do your heart good to be in our tent to hear our songs and our cheery conversation. . . . We are very near the end. . . . We did intend to finish ourselves when things proved like this, but we have decided to die naturally without.[7]

Where did they get that courage? How could they sing songs and carry on cheerful conversation? And where did Daniel get it or Sir Thomas More or Sojourner Truth? They got it from God who has created us to be virtuous people and gives us the strength to be.

It will not be easy, it never is, to stand for righteousness in the personal realm and social realm, but God gives strength to those who try. Jesus Christ who showed us God's face said: "In the world you have tribulation; but be of good cheer, I have overcome the world" (John 16:33).

This is the courage-making vision that has led the people of God through persecution and contempt. These people "desitute, afflicted, ill-treated—of whom the world was not worthy" (Heb. 11:37-38) have kept on in faith, journeying toward that "city which has foundations, whose builder and maker is God" (v. 10).

May this same God give you the courage to be who you were created to be and to make a difference for righteousness in our world today.

### Notes

1.   Bernard Haring, *The Law of Christ* (Westminister Maryland: Neuman Press, 1961), vol. 3, p. 34.

2.   P. T. Geach, *The Virtues*, p. 160.

3.   Robert Bolt, *A Man For All Seasons*, p. 140.

4.   Ibid., pp. 140-141.

5.   Cited in Bill J. Leonard, *Word of God Across the Ages* (Nashville: Broadman Press, 1981), p. 71.

6.   Paul Tillich, *The Courage to Be* (New Haven: Yale University Press, 1952), p. 3.

7.   J. M. Barrie, *Courage* (London: Hodder and Stoughton, 1922), p. 31.

# 12
# Justice

Now we investigate the virtue called justice. Paul said, "Whatsoever things are just, . . . think on these things" (Phil. 4:8, KJV).

Most of us have some idea of what justice means. You discovered it the first time your sister got a bigger piece of the cake than you did. We all have been supplied by God with a gismo inside of us called a "fairness meter." Anytime anybody gets more than we do, an alarm goes off and it screams: "No fair!" It is a very delicate instrument; it takes very little to set it off. It has been designed by God to measure unfairness to others as well as the self but by a peculiar quirk in our nature we call sin, we tend to pay attention to the meter only when the unfairness has been done to us.

God has not withheld a sense of justice from any person. In his Roman letter Paul observed that the Gentiles have a law written on their hearts—their conscience bears witness to God's law (2:14-15); and one part of God's law has to do with justice. Justice is a common or natural grace given to all. It is a civic virtue; on it the survival of the nation depends. As Walter Rauschenbusch said, "Nations die of legalized injustice."

As you go into Notre Dame, the virtue of justice is pictured in sculpture as a woman holding a set of scales. That should be familiar to you; the blindfolded woman holding the scales of justice has long been an American symbol for justice. If it were only true. Too often the woman peeks through the blindfold; or, if she doesn't, somebody has their hands on the scales tipping it in somebody's favor.

## I

What is this justice of which we all have some dim awareness but which is so rarely realized in our lives?

Plato and Aristotle defined justice according to the slogan "Every man his due." Thomas Aquinas drawing upon the classical tradition defined this virtue as "The firm and unchanging will to give to each one his due."

The problem with this definition is that it doesn't go far enough and thereby has tended to sanctify a rigid class structure. "To every man his due," yes, but kings were due one thing, philosophers another, women another, and slaves another. In other words, it defended inequality as a divine necessity. Their logic went something like this: If God did not mean for kings to live in luxury, He wouldn't have given them palaces.

The biblical notion of justice is deeper and truer than the classical that tradition gave us.

## II

The biblical notion of justice is founded upon the great concept of righteousness. Justice is the "righteousing" power of God in our lives and in our history which is at work setting things right and creating healed relationships, healed communities, and a healed earth. It manifests itself in personal righteousness and social righteousness.

In Old Testament and Hebrew tradition, the great hero of justice was Joseph. In Jewish tradition he is called Tzaddik, the Just. If Abraham is the hero of faith, Moses the hero of Exodus and Law, Solomon the hero of wisdom, and Daniel the hero of courage, Joseph is known as the hero of righteousness. Joseph the Just: The beautiful melding of personal and social righteousness.

Why is Joseph called Tzaddik, the Just? Because he exhibited personal righteousness. He would not tell lies; he resisted Madame Potiphar's seduction; he was able to forgive his brothers for selling him into slavery; and he kept his promise not to hurt his brothers.

Here are marks of personal righteousness. **Telling the truth.** A recent sociologist estimated that the average American tells 200 lies per day. Lying has become a way of life. We think little lies do no harm, but soon this habit so corrupts our souls that it becomes easy to tell big ones. We are taught that in exceptional cases—to save life, for example—lying is permissible, but we use the exceptional cases to justify lying in any case. Righteousness is that power of God that makes all relationships healthy. Relationships die when lies dominate the truth.

**Sexual morality.** Righteousness in sexual morality is based upon covenant faithfulness: Keeping faithful to your own spouse and not luring others into being unfaithful to theirs.

**Power to forgive.** Justice without mercy is too harsh, too demanding, uncreative, life-denying. As Reinhold Neibuhr said, "Any justice which is only justice soon degenerates into something less than justice. It must be saved by something which is more than justice." That something more is love. True righteousness is justice tempered with mercy.

**Keeping promises.** Joseph promised his father not to wreak revenge on his brothers. Even when father Jacob died, Joseph still kept his promise, a mark of personal righteousness.

But Joseph the Just also exhibited social righteousness. He was an able prince. As the king's right-hand man, he administered justice fairly and promoted the welfare of the people. He helped the nation prepare for the famine, and when it came he led Egypt to feed not only its own but also all those from surrounding countries who came for food. He exhibited the true righteousness God wants from rulers. As the psalmist says, "Give the king thy justice, O God" (Ps. 72:1).

## III

Another hero of justice was the prophet Amos.

His first—and maybe last—sermon was an unforgettable scene. It was the most high and holy day for the nation of Israel: the yearly celebration at Bethel. On this day the people worshiped at the shrine of civil religion. It was the wedding of patriotism and religion. The state and church joined arms to sing "God bless our Israel." They had good reason to be happy. It was eighth-century Israel, the height of military strength and economic prosperity that the Northern Kingdom would ever reach. Jereboam II was rating high marks in the polls and Wall Street was happy.

It was like Inauguration Day in America. The president was there, and so were the priests and the poets, the prayers and the music.

Into this celebration walked an unknown, poorly dressed migrant farmer. Known only as "Amos [of] the shepherds of Tekoa," he walked in like Caesar Chavez, crashing an inauguration to deliver his message from God.

The crowd was confused and nervous at first—what would this rude intruder say? But soon their anxiety gave way to approval and applause. For Amos began announcing God's judgment on the enemies of Israel. (That will preach!) Thus says the Lord:

"For the sins of Damascus I will punish them," says the Lord.

*Amen* went the senators.

"For the sins of Gaza I will destroy them"

*Amen* went the judges.

"For the sins of Tyre I will send proper punishments."

*Amen* cried the moral majority.

"For the sins of Edom and Ammon I will repay," says the Lord.

*Amen* cried the whole crowd, breaking into spontaneous applause. "This preacher may be a bit scruffy-looking, but he knows how to preach!"

Then as they leaned forward, licking their lips in anticipation for the next denunciationi from the Lord, Amos let them have it between the eyes.

"For the sins of Israel, for your sins, God will punish you."

In stunned silence, the crowd listened. Amos went on:

"You sell your righteousness for cash. You buy and sell the needy for a measly pair of sandals. You trample the heads of the poor into the dust."

Then he looked out at the sea of $10,000 gowns, top hats, and tuxedos and said: "You lie on ivory beds while people are cold and lonely."

He looked at the overnourished women and said: "You cows of Bashan, you sit around and say 'Bring me more to drink,' while people starve."

He turned to the judges and said: "Your courts of law are a sham. The famous and rich get preferential treatment; the poor and forgotten get no justice at all."

He said: "You've been crooked so long you don't know what straight is. Let me show you a straight line. I saw the Lord in a dream. He was standing beside a wall built with a plumb line with a plumb line in his hand and he said, 'Amos, what do you see?' and I said, 'A plumb line,' and He said, 'This plumb line I now set in the midst of my people.'"

Only God's Word can set us straight.

Then Amos turned to the religious folk in the crowd, the preachers and the churchgoers, and gave an even harder word:

"You come to church and use my name but you ignore the needs of your neighbor. You have religion but you don't have love."

"For that reason I despise your covered-dish suppers and worship services. When you take up offerings I turn my head; you sing hymns but they are like noise to my ears.

"Here is what I want: 'Let justice roll down like waters, and righteousness like an everflowing stream.'"

God was saying what He would say again and again through His prophets: "I don't want lavish ceremony; I want right living."

Sydney Harris wrote recently a comment that evoked bushels of negative mail. He said: God could do well with less praise from his children and more imitation. No wonder. Recent Gallup Polls report that while religion is on the rise, morality is in decline. Gallup revealed that there is very little difference found in the behavior of the churched and unchurched on a wide range of issues including lying, cheating, and stealing.[1]

Here is what concerns God most: Not elaborate ritual, not even perfect doctrine, but right living.

"Let justice roll down like waters, and righteousness like an everflowing stream" (Amos 5:24).

"Like waters, . . . like an everflowing stream." A remarkable image. God's justice and righteousness are the life-giving streams of society. They replenish the barren land. Like an everflowing stream, they must come—not like the flood waters that periodically wash in and rush over a parched land, causing ruin, never soaking into the ground. Like an everflowing stream.

Implicit in the image is a warning of judgment. Like an everflowing stream God's justice must flow. When we block up the flowing waters of justice with the dam of our greed and prejudice and selfishness then the earth begins to wither. The waters heap up dark and furious against the walls of the dam until finally they break through, destroying the dam, the torrential waters pouring over the land causing destruction. When this happens, God's justice has become judgment and His righteousness has turned into wrath.

Like an everflowing stream. God needs more than ritualistic kindness: Fruit baskets at Christmas. Along with charity God wants justice. A Christmas bonus is no substitute for a living wage.

"Let justice roll down like waters and righteousness like an everflowing stream."

Remember a few years back when the media publicized the famine in Central Africa: Our compassion moved us to send thousands of tons of grain, such huge quantities in such a short span of time that the grain spoiled and rotted in the loading docks.

Justice: Like rolling waters it needs to be, like an everflowing stream.

What is justice; what is righteousness? Naming them is risky and necessary.

It is personal righteousness—living by the Ten Commandments and the Sermon on the Mount. It is doing unto others as you would have them do to you. And it is social righteousness: racial justice, equal rights before the law for women, fairness in the courts, protection for the weak and disabled; opportunity for honest work for anybody who will. It is care of the earth; it is conscientious negotiation toward the ending of the nuclear arms race. These are marks of God's righteousness. They need far more than every fourth-year splurges of concern. They need constant, patient, persistent care. Like an everflowing stream.

### IV

Now we turn to justice in American politics. In the 1984 election, both political parties claimed to be instruments of God's righteousness. Each champions a part of what justice is, but both parties are far from the goal of biblical justice. Neither the parties nor the American people have a real hunger or thirst for righteousness.

In a modern democratic society real justice is kept alive by the creative collaboration of two great but conflicting ideals: freedom and equality. These ideals are not the same. They are two opposite ideals which keep each other honest and between them make for justice.

The genius of American politics is to be found in the dynamic interplay of the two impulses of freedom and equality.

The freedom impulse says that justice happens when people get the full rewards of their labors. It is a celebration of achievement. The government should not interfere. It is one interpretation of "every man his due." This is a noble ideal but we should not fail to recognize the danger of its logical extreme:

the law of the jungle, the law of tooth and claw, the survival of the fittest, social Darwinism. The cruel outcome of the impulse of freedom untempered by equality is a society where the strong get stronger and the weak get weaker, where the poor get poorer and the rich get religious. What begins in a noble idea ends in Fascism and institutionalized injustice.

Now lets look at the other side: the impulse of equality. This side says that justice has to do not only with just rewards but also just opportunity. It celebrates egalitarianism; it proposes a more just distribution of the nations resources so that everybody gets a fairer share of the American dream. The American dream is founded not only on "Life, Liberty and the pursuit of Happiness' but on the notion that "all men are created equal" and therefore everyone should be given equal opportunity in health and education, in the personnel office, and in the courts. It says that a nation's righteousness has to do with how it treats its weaker and poorer citizens.

This is a noble ideal, but unless it is tempered by the ideal of freedom, its logical extreme ends up in the enforced equality of Communism. That is equality without freedom.

The genius of our ideal is that we believe we can be both just and free, that freedom and equality are partners in the path toward justice.

It may be dawning on you that at this moment in our history one political party is the champion of the freedom impulse and the other party is the champion of the equality impulse. And if that were not enough to polarize the parties, they also have embodied the polarity of personal versus social righteousness. One party is championing personal righteousness—anti-abortion, prayer in school, and so forth; the other party is championing social righteousness—care for the poor, peace making, and so forth.

What we are witnessing is a growing polarization of these two camps. We are becoming two Americas, a freedom party and an equality party, a personal righteousness party and a social righteousness party. And what is even more alarming is that we also may be becoming a nation of two churches, a freedom church and an equality church, a conservative coalition church and a rainbow coalition church.

I can see it now, I don't know whether it is a nightmare or a comedy, all American denominations have been reduced to two: The first is called the American Evangelical Church. Its denominational headquarters is located in Nashville, Tennessee. In worship, instead of the doxology they sing the "Star-Spangled Banner" and over the altar is inscribed "Life, Liberty, and the Pursuit of Happiness."

The second church is called The People's Church of America. Its denominational headquarters alternate (to be fair) among New York City, San Francisco, and Miami. In its worship there is inscribed over the altar the words, "All persons are created equal" and instead of the Apostles' Creed, they recite together this creed: We Believe Everything.

It is intellectually and politically dangerous to so polarize the ideals of freedom and equality that we no longer recognize that either one alone is corrupting and that if either party adopts one alone it is corrupted. It is dangerous for either party to claim that it is the instrument of God's righteousness. The biblical word for that is *blasphemy*.

And it is spiritually dangerous for a church to identify God's will with either party; the biblical word for that is *idolatry*. If that happens then we will no longer be a nation of religious freedom and religious pluralism but a nation of two political religions: the religion of freedom and the religion of equality.

Justice will suffer when the creative collaboration of freedom and equality turns into a war of political religions. And the church? It will have not only have sold its soul for a porridge of power, it will have invited a deep split in every congregation and denomination in America.

I have a dream of an America where justice rolls down like waters and righteousness like an everflowing stream; where we can be both free and equal; where we will be smart enough to look beyond self-interest to the common good; where we will discover that it is politically expedient to be generous to our poor at home and around the world; where weapons production will no longer dominate any nation's economy; where greed will not corrupt the powerful, injure the powerless, and destroy the earth; where race, sex, and class will be no barrier for any person; where industry will provide enough jobs for everybody; and where we can fight evil without becoming evil and do good without becoming self-righteous.

That is the gift offered to us by God, for justice is an evidence of grace, the "righteousing" power of God to set right all that is wrong and to create healed relationships, a healed community and a healed earth.

Get out there folks and make some justice—God's kind of justice.

**Note**
1. *The Louisville Times* (Friday July 13, 1984, A16).

FOR GOD DID NOT GIVE US A SPIRIT OF TIMIDITY, BUT A SPIRIT OF POWER AND LOVE AND TEMPERANCE ✝ THE FRUIT OF THE SPIRIT IS TEMPERANCE

self-control

# 13
# Temperance

I have quite an ambitious goal for this chapter: to get you to love temperance. Of all the virtues, it is least loved and most ridiculed.

Paul told us to consider what is morally excellent. When my secretary first typed that phrase, "morally excellent," she added a "t" so it read *"mortally* excellent"—reminding me of a title I read somewhere on the virtues called "The Seven Deadly Virtues." I suppose that could particularly apply to the popular conception of temperance. It seems so life-denying when in fact temperance is a lovely virtue, indispensable for moral excellence. P. T. Geach said, "Nobody can safely settle for a mediocre degree of virtue." Christ surely has not called us to mediocrity in virtue. Grace should not make us morally sloppy. Jesus said, "Be perfect—just as your Father in heaven is perfect" (Matt. 5:28, GNB). Temperance may be your missing ingredient to moral excellence.

I suppose the first rule for a chapter on temperance is that it not speak intemperantly of temperance. In the comic strip "The Wizard of Id" the preacher is waxing eloquent on the great virtue of temperance, or moderation, as it is sometimes named. He exclaims, "Moderation is the key to living. Follow the Golden Mean. Eat moderation, drink moderation, sleep moderation, work moderation, play moderation, live moderation." On and on he went. After the service the king passed by in the foyer, shook hands with the preacher, and said: "I think you overdid it."

The ancient maxim for temperance was this: *Nothing overmuch,* and that should apply to temperance itself. Part of the reason this virtue is so despised and ridiculed is so many people have been intemperate in support of temperance, so immoderate in search of moderation. In truth, temperance is a lovely virtue. It is tragic that some people have turned it into a prideful abstinence or joyless asceticism, for these pervert both classical and biblical notions. What is the lovely virtue of temperance?

# I

The Greek ideal of temperance is of the well-ordered soul, the well-balanced self, the well-proportioned life.

Plato said that temperance was the rational ordering of the soul that kept it free. The animal or natural vitalities must be governed, he said, lest they produce "a feverish state in the soul, a city of pigs" which knows no limits. The ungoverned soul, he said, is like the State ruled by cooks, bakers, tap dancers, and flute-girls.[1]

The vitalities or appetites have their place but should not rule. Plato contrasted the role of the cook with the role of the physician. The cook ministers to what the body wants; the physician to what the body needs. Boston cream cake is not bad; it just has its proper place. Temperance then is not the elimination of natural appetites as evil; it is the proper ordering of what is good.

Aristotle was the champion of the golden mean—moderation in everything. Temperance was for him a chief virtue; indeed it was the prerequisite of every virtue. Courage, for example, was the mean between cowardice on one extreme and rashness on the other. "Nothing overmuch" is the maxim of moderation, or in Milton's words, "The rule of not too much by temperance taught."

Now let us look at some specifics. Since this chapter is on the virtue, not the vice, I will not major on the vices, but a few negative examples are necessary.

In both classical and biblical texts gluttony and drunkenness are mentioned as twin enemies of temperance. They always go together—"gluttony and drunkenness"—like soup and sandwich or horse and carriage or love and marriage. Both represent a filling of the body to compensate for spiritual emptiness. In one Latin text, five kinds of gluttony are enumerated in five adverbs: eating too quickly, too eagerly, too much, too expensively, and too fussily. Drunkenness is the loss of self in the bottle. Whether by occasional excess or daily use, it is the blurring and giving up of the self through inebriation.

Only we should not stop there. Temperance also means moderation in physical exercise and sports. *Eutrapelia* is the name Aristotle and Aquinas used for that excess. Or moderation in temper: A person quick to anger is intemperate. Aristotle warned that even the pleasure of learning can be pursued intemperately. I recently read the true story of a lover of books who went overboard. He turned form a bibliophile to a bibliomaniac. He became obsessed with the goal of owning a copy of every book ever written. First, books lined every wall, then they began to pile up from the floor to ceiling all over the rooms. Soon he moved his wife into the garage so he could have more room inside. She suffered a breakdown and was institutionalized. He should have been.

In all these examples you see the self taken over by an impulse or desire. The self is being ruled by part of the self. Socrates compared the intemperate man to a vessel full of holes because it can never be satisfied. Haunted by inner emptiness, the self grasps for something to fill itself with. So the self becomes intemperate, compulsive in food (gluttony) or drink (alcoholism) or work (workaholism[2]) or sex (promiscuity).

Or, the self does not know itself and so it is pulled in all directions at once. One excess does not ruin it; it is the excess of many things pulling it apart. This kind of person cannot say no and cannot set priorities. In the classical ideal, the soul was rationally able to order properly all pleasures and desires. In Plato's *The Republic*, Socrates says that there is in the human soul "a better and worse principle." When the better has the worse under control, he said, then a man is master of himself.

You are beginning to see the difference between the spirit of temperance and the spirit of asceticism. The spirit of temperance sees all of God's creation as good, but, at the same time, sees the need to order natural appetites and desires in order to stay free and be productive. The spirit of asceticism, on the other hand, sees the natural world as evil and despises it. Its path is not temperance, but abstinence. Abstinence may be necessary for you to be temperate in a certain area, but it is not the rule. Aristotle said that the path of temperance is different for everybody. The amount of food an athlete consumes preparing for the Olympics may be temperate for him, but not for the average person. And poverty and chastity may be temperate for the monk married to God, but not for the average person.

Let me draw a picture of intemperance.

A person told me once: "My life is an emotional roller coaster. I go up and down from one extreme to another. I wish I could find some equilibrium." That is one kind of intemperance.

Another person says, "I feel pulled in all different directions. I run from one thing to another. I cannot set priorities."

Henri Nouwen calls this "the compulsive self." Our calendars are filled to the brim, we are driven with frantic busyness. We have a false self shaped by our culture and so are compulsively, treacherously busy.

The compulsive self works too much, talks too much, drinks too much, eats too much, worries too much. Unsure of its identity, the false self is pushed to and fro by the world. Scared of emptiness, the compulsive self rushes to fill itself with something, anything.

The temperate person knows who he or she is and is not driven to satisfy a false self—or a menagerie of false selves. The temperate self knows what is important, has discovered the "rule of better and worse" and is willing to set priorities. The temperate person sets goals and is willing to sacrifice for what he or she wants. *Wanting*, in its primitive meaning, means *trying to get*. All of us say we want things we aren't really trying to get. A student told her professor she wanted to be a medical doctor. The professor asked what she was taking this semester. Yoga, Sanskrit, and English literature. Any biology? No. Any organic chemistry? No. That person had a gap between what she said she wanted to be and what she was willing to do to achieve that goal. An athlete living on cigarettes and gin and cocaine doesn't really want to be a class athlete. A temperate person makes wise judgments about what needs to be done (and not to be done) in order to achieve life's goals.

Freud was speaking about temperance when he said that the ego must move from the pleasure principle to the reality principle. The pleasure principle is the infantile stage of development where we must have all our desires met. In the reality principle stage, the ego is willing to forego immediate gratification to achieve life's goals.

We have many people today stuck in the pleasure principle. Dr. Dan Kiley has identified a malady (epidemic I would say) among contemporary American males in *The Peter Pan Syndrome*.[3] Men in the Peter Pan Syndrome refuse to grow up. They are narcissistic and irresponsible. They covet intimacy to a point but are unwilling to make commitments and sustain long-term relationships. On the surface they appear normal, but underneath they are anxious and lonely. Christopher Lasch has identified such a life-style as characteristic of American life as a whole in his provocative *The Culture of Narcissism*.[4] Contemporary America is a culture of people craving instant gratification, denying authority, exalting the self, and rejecting discipline. Temperance has become a forgotten virtue.

Temperance is the order of the soul that is willing to choose, make commitments, forego immediate gratification, and set priorities. This is the natural grace; the civic virtue called temperance. We cannot really be happy without it.

## II

In the Bible the main word for temperance is *self-control.*
Two proverbs illustrate:

> A man without self-control [he that hath no rule over his own
> spirit—KJV] is like a city broken into and left without walls
> (Prov. 25:28).
> He who is slow to anger is better than the mighty, and he who
> rules his spirit than he who takes a city (Prov. 16:32).

In the New Testament, the word in the Greek means self-
control too: the well-ordered soul. But there are two distinc-
tions between the classical and biblical ideal of Temperance.
Both speak of ordering the soul or self. But the Greek ideal is
of the well-proportioned soul, well-balanced soul—much like a
well-proportioned body. In the biblical ideal, the soul is ordered
toward love—the love of God and neighbor. Temperance is not
for its own sake, but for God's sake and the neighbor's. In other
words, it is fulfilled in love. You tune your body and soul for the
sake of the kingdom and its righteousness.

The other distinction is just as crucial. The Greek believed
that the mind could conquer all life's problems. The root of all
evil was ignorance; reason can save us. So temperance was the
rational ordering of the soul. But the Bible goes deeper. The
root of all evil is sin, a deep distortion of the heart, and reason
alone cannot save us. So in the Bible the source of temperance
is not reason; it is the Spirit of God. Reason can take care of
ignorance, but only the power of God can overcome sin. In the
Bible temperance is the Spirit-filled life: "The fruit of the Spirit
is . . . temperance" (Gal. 5:22-23).

It is God who through His Spirit orders our souls. When we
bow and worship Him, we find order within. When He is Lord,
everything else takes its rightful place. In the Bible, salvation
is not the absence of desire, it is the proper ordering of desire.
Temperance is not the absence of passion; it is the transfigura-
tion of passion into wholeness.

Jesus was speaking of temperance when He said "Seek ye

first the kingdom of God, ... and all these things shall be added unto you" (Matt. 6:33, KJV), and also when He said, "No one can serve two masters" (v. 24). Temperance is not letting a part of the self or some part of creation become Lord of self. When Christ is Lord, nothing else can be; when He is not Lord, anything can be. When you seek first the kingdom, all these other things will find their rightful place.

The witness of the New Testament is that the Spirit of God produces wholeness, and that this Spirit brings self-control.

The most familiar passage is in Galatians 5:16-25 where Paul contrasts walking according to the flesh and walking according to the Spirit. It pictures temperance versus intemperance.

To walk according to the flesh, means that a part of the self, a part of God's good created reality, has become Lord of the self. Things are out of kilter. Some things in the natural created realm have taken over. Evidences of walking according to the flesh are enumerated: fornication, impurity, licentiousness, idolatry, sorcery, enmity, strife, jealousy, anger, selfishness, dissension, party spirit, envy, drunkenness, and carousing.

But to walk according to the Spirit, is to walk as a well-ordered soul, a self oriented toward wholeness, a person organized for love. Evidences of this grace are love, joy, peace, patience, kindness, goodness, faithfulness, gentleness, and self-control.

Paul uses a curious phrase: "Against such there is no law" (v. 23). What he is saying is that true temperance is a gift of the Spirit more than a work of the law. The law can force an ordering of the soul; but this ordering is not able to control the unruly human spirit for long. Even as a society under martial law is a pretty grim affair, so is the human spirit controlled only by laws and rules.

The loveliness of Christian temperance is that it is a gift of the Spirit and as such is realized in joyful obedience, not grim obligation.

We have been given the power of virtue; the mystery of goodness has dawned on our hearts. So the Scripture says:

"Hence I remind you to rekindle the gift of God that is within you . . . for God did not give us a spirit of timidity but a spirit of power and love and self-control" (2 Tim. 1:6-7). How would you like that power?

Temperance is an evidence of grace, the grace of a well-ordered soul, a self organized to love, the grace of Christ-in-us.

### III

Look at the life of Christ. The way of Jesus was not joyless abstinence but lovely temperance. He was one who enjoyed life and all its good gifts but kept them in their rightful place. He rejected the grim asceticism of John the Baptist; He enjoyed dinner parties and good friendships and extravagant gifts. But when the time came He was willing to let go of everything for the sake of the kingdom. His kind of temperance was not the denial of life but rather the affirmation of an abundant life organized for love.

The person said, "My life was an emotional roller coaster until I gave it to Christ. He has given my life stability." Another said, "When Christ came into my life, everything fell into the right groove. It felt right."

Christ comes to reorder your soul so that it is happy, responsible, and free. When you invite Him into your life, the Spirit of God dwells in you.

You have been created in the image of Christ; He is your secret self, the truest truth about who you are. This real self gets overlaid by many layers of false selves; your true self stays a secret even from you. When you receive Christ and invite Him to be Savior, Lord, and Friend, you get in touch with your true self. Because you know who you are, the compulsions of the false self fade away. When Christ is Lord, then all the good desires and appetites God has given us find their rightful place and stay as good as God made them.

When Christ comes into your life, He will help you organize your life according to the love of God and neighbor. That is your true happiness for that is your reason for being.

When Christ's Spirit dwells in you, you will decide what to do and not to do, what to give up and to keep, not by anybody else's set code, but by what is right for you. Then you will live obedient and free—not because you have to, but because you want to. Then your temperance will take on a joyful character. Then you will see how "lovely" temperance is.

What struggles of the soul are you having? What habits do you need to break? Is your soul always in a feverish scramble? Wouldn't you love to find stability within? Come, receive Christ, and let the power of His love order your soul. This was the yearning of John Greenleaf Whittier when he wrote this hymn:

> Dear Lord, and Father of mankind,
>     Forgive our foolish ways;
> Reclothe us in our rightful mind;
> In purer lives thy service find,
>     In deeper reverence, praise.
>
> Drop thy still dews of quietness,
>     Till all our strivings cease;
> Take from our souls the strain and stress,
> And let our ordered lives confess
>     The beauty of Thy peace.

### Notes

1. Karl A. Olsson, *Seven Sins and Seven Virtues* (New York: Harper & Brothers, 1959), p. 95.
2. The term "workaholic" was coined by Wayne Oates in his *Confessions of a Workaholic* (New York: World Publishing, 1971).
3. Dan Kiley, *The Peter Pan Syndrome* (New York: Dodd, Mead & Co., 1983).
4. Christopher Lasch, *The Culture of Narcissism: American Life in an Age of Diminishing Expectations* (New York: W. W. Norton & Company, 1978).

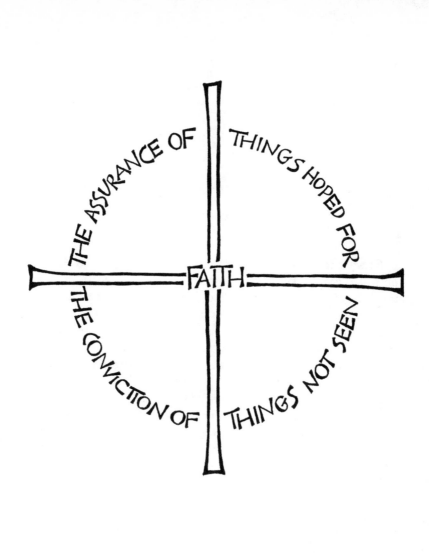

# 14
# Faith

*Everyone doubts.* This seems an odd way to begin a sermon on faith. Everybody doubts something, sometime. If not, they need to get their glands checked. Bring in the endocrinologist, this person is unreal! Doubt is not the opposite of faith. The opposite of faith is despair or smugness. In fact, the presence of doubt is itself a proof of faith, for faith is no sure thing. It is living life open-eyed in the face of life's ambiguity and darkness. It is as Hebrews says, "The assurance of things hoped for, the conviction of things not seen" (11:1). Blaise Pascal, brilliant seventeenth-century scientist and famous convert to Christianity, said that faith is always a wager, but a wager with the best odds: If you lose, you lose nothing important, but if you win, you gain everything.[1]

The apostle Paul said that we move "from faith to faith." We move from one level of faith to another. Doubt is what keeps our faith moving from a less adequate faith to a more adequate one. When a person tells me she has doubts, I more often than not say, "Good for you!' That means you have outgrown an old, inadequate faith and you are searching for a new more adequate one." In J. B. Phillips's book *Your God Is Too Small,* he described notions of God too small for a mature faith in a modern world. Doubts stir us to move from too small a God to one more adequate for our lives.

Frederick Buechner said: "Doubts are the ants in the pants of faith. They keep it awake and moving."[2] Everybody doubts.

## I

*Everyone believes.* That sounds better, huh? Well, let's see. Everybody believes in something. Faith is a way of organizing your life. If you don't believe in God and organize your life around God, you will believe in something else; you will believe in self, or in science, or in America, or in progress, or in the astrological charts, or in positive thinking, or in "love, sweet love." Even atheists believe in something, if only in their own atheism. Slogans like "Keep the faith" or "Believe it can happen" are used in everything from rock songs to self-help books to basketball tournaments to political campaigns. You need a measure of faith to keep going even if you're not sure what you believe in. "Believe in something, even if it is wrong," some suggest. Dare we take such a risk? Misplaced faith, faith in the wrong things, can lead to destruction or to despair. People had faith in Jim Jones, and he led them to Guyana where they drank a poisoned beverage and died. And faith in self or in progress or in "the goodness of mankind" can be rudely contradicted by our limitations and other's. Despair lurks just around the corner.

## II

So we come to the crux of the matter. Faith is only as good as what or whom you have faith in. Christianity offers faith in a supremely good and gracious God revealed by Jesus of Nazareth. This God has acted in history to speak His "yes" to you. That is grace. When we by faith say our "yes" back to God, we are moved into a relationship with God that brings us wholeness, meaning, and confidence.

A definition. Faith is the response of the whole person to the power and love of God which moves us into personal relationship with God and into participation in His Kingdom and its community.

If faith is the offering of the whole person to God, it is an act of the mind, heart, and will. It is, therefore, *belief,* an act of the mind, *trust,* an act of the heart, and *obedience,* an act of the will. Jesus suggested such by summarizing God's law as the love of God with all your heart, mind, and strength. And so Richard of Chichester formed his thirteenth-century prayer, adapted for us in the contemporary Broadway musical *Godspell:*

"Day by day, O Lord, three things I pray,
to see thee more clearly (the mind)
to love thee more dearly (the heart)
to follow thee more nearly (the will)."

## III

Faith demands the assent of the mind and as such is a kind of knowledge. In John's Gospel, Jesus prayed, "And this is eternal life, that they know thee the only true God, and Jesus Christ whom thou has sent" (17:3).

This is the dimension of faith we call *belief.* Beliefs, confessions, creeds, theological affirmations are all what Karl Barth called "faith seeking understanding." Sometimes faith is used as "the faith," which refers to a body of beliefs we affirm as Christians.

It is important what you believe. As I said earlier, believing in the wrong things can lead to destruction and despair. Moreover, bad theology issues into bad living (as bad living constructs its own bad theology). A person who believes in salvation by works—that we must earn our salvation—will likely become a workaholic or churchaholic, a person compulsively driven to save oneself by a never-finished list of accomplishments, good deeds, or worthwhile activities. Flannery O'Conner says that we act out our heresies dramatically.[3] How right she is.

For me, a list of essential right things to believe in order to have a faith that brings wholeness includes the following:

1. God is a loving parent who is Creator of all that is.
2. Creation is the good act of God and we human beings are

God's children, the crown of His creation, created in God's own image.

3. The image of God in which we were made is the capacity to live in communion with God and in community with neighbor. As we live in such communion and community, we fulfill our calling as God's children and become God's partners in the flourishing of His world.

4. Though we were created good, we pervert our true nature through sin which is anything that separates us from God and from one another and anything which destroys God's world.

5. Jesus Christ is the Son of God who has come to earth to show us what God is like and what it means to be fully human. His life and death reconciles us who were estranged from God to God. This reconciliation is not something we can earn but is a gift—what we call grace.

6. God is at work in all history to bring His world to a victorious close. Easter is a foretaste of the final victory of life over death and love over hate. The means God has chosen to adopt in the pursuing of this final victory is the way of love, a nonviolent, servant love which in history becomes a suffering love, a love eloquent in its suffering and powerful to redeem the human heart and all existence.

7. By His Spirit God calls people like you and me to be His partners in this redemptive plan. If by faith we join Him, we are what the Bible calls "saved" which means "made whole" and refers to restored communion with God and community with others.

When your mind says yes to such things as the aforementioned, you will believe in the biblical God revealed in Jesus Christ. You will live much better if you do.

## IV

But faith is more than an act of the mind, it is also an act of the heart and as such it is *trust*. The mind believes, but only the heart trusts. Trust is a deeper dimension of faith than beliefs. We can argue over beliefs and we will certainly change or modify a few of them as we go along. Trust, however, is the deeper intuition of faith that places your life in the care of another.

The trapeze artist strung a line across Niagara Falls and proceeded to push a wheelbarrow across it. The crowd applauded. "How many of you think I can push another person across in the wheelbarrow?" he asked. The crowd raised their hands. "Who would volunteer to go with me?" The hands ducked for cover. Such is the difference between "believing that . . ." and "trusting in. . . ."

Faith is the response of the heart to the God who has been revealed to us in Jesus Christ. Pascal said,

> The heart has its reasons, which reason does not know. It is the heart which experiences God, and not the reason. This, then is faith: God felt by the heart, not by the reason. . . . The knowledge of God is very far from the love of him . . .[4]

When faith begins, we are somehow moved by God's majesty and mystery and love, and we respond by trusting in Him. In the wild beating of the heart, sometimes with a lump in the throat too big to swallow, often with a sense of risk because like marriage the faith decision is the offering of our lives to another person whom we cannot perfectly know and with no guarantees for the future, we entrust our lives to the goodness and graciousness of God.

We cannot prove our trust, just as we cannot prove our trust in a marriage partner or friend. And to force the other person to prove their worthiness would spoil the relationship and be itself a sign of mistrust.[5] Faith simply trusts, trusts at a deeper level than the mind can believe or prove.

## V

Faith finally is an act of the will and as such is *obedience*. If you want to see someone's faith, look where their feet take them, watch how they relate to children, study their check stubs. "Faith without works is dead," said James (2:17, KJV), and he was fighting some people's notion of faith that had to do with the rightness of what they believe or the sincerity of their hearts but did not include how they live.

Dietrich Bonhoeffer, German theologian and martyr under Hitler, said unswervingly, "Only he who believes is obedient, and only he who is obedient believes."[6] Some people aren't too clear about what their minds believe, their hearts are not always glowing with trust either, but they are absolutely steadfast in living the responsible life faithful to what God commands. This person is a person of faith.

Sometimes our minds lead out in faith and we wait for our hearts and wills to catch up. C. S. Lewis said, "Faith is the art of holding onto things your reason has once accepted, in spite of your changing moods."[7] Sometimes our hearts lead the way, and our minds struggle to make sense of it all. Often, however, we need to change our behavior before our minds and hearts can come along. To those who wanted to believe but could not, Pascal advised to *act as if* they believed and believing would follow.[8] Sometimes our minds and hearts are just waiting for our bodies to get serious and kick into action. A man named Bridges once wrote the poet/mystic Gerard Manley Hopkins and asked how he could possibly learn to believe, expecting some soaring metaphysical answer. Hopkins only replied: "Give alms."[9]

Faith is the response of the whole person to God—mind, heart, and will. It is belief, trust, and obedience. To withhold any of the three is to stunt the growth of your faith.

## VI

Faith is such an offering of yourself to God, but again I emphasize it is no sure thing. It has the audacity to believe in an invisible God, to trust in an unproveable truth, and to follow a path whose destination is not yet in sight. Faith is not, as one suggested, a journey without maps, however, it never has the full map in its hands as it journeys.

Hebrews says it well: "Faith is the assurance of things hoped for, the conviction of things not seen" (11:1).

Faith gives to us the virtue of *faithfulness,* the determination to stick with it and keep on keeping on, never giving up on God's commands or on God's final victory. Faith makes us faithful.

Faith also gives us *confidence.* Convictions build confidence, and confidence keeps us going in life through all its ups and downs.

The eleventh chapter of Hebrews provides a roll call of heroes and heroines of faith.

There is Noah building an absurd contraption called an "ark" simply because God commanded him to and warned there would be a great flood. He was hammering away long before the clouds had formed or the drops had begun to fall.

There is Abraham who by faith picked up his family and possessions and journeyed to an unknown country. And there he was still believing and there his wife Sarah was still believing in God's promise to give them a child, even though he was 100 and she was 90. Even to try to have children at that age is an incredible act of faith. When the angel let them in on the news that they were expecting, Abraham and Sarah fell over laughing (Had she thought the morning sickness was a bad case of the flu?), and they named their child Isaac, which means "laughter." Faith is the laughter of those who see the promises of God fulfilled.

We could add to the list: The midwives who refused to follow Pharaoh's command to kill the boy babies and, instead, followed God. Without them Moses would not have lived to fulfill God's purpose.

Faith is the stuff inside of three Hebrew boys dragged off into Babylonian captivity, Shadrach, Meshach, and Abednego, who refused under threat of being thrown into a fiery furnace to worship Babylonian gods. Brought before King Nebuchadnezzar, they said: "If it be so, our God whom we serve is able to deliver us from the burning fiery furnace. . . . But if not, be it known to you, O king, that we will not serve your gods" (Dan. 3:17-18).

On faith's honor roll are prophets who spoke God's word no matter the consequence and women who kept the faith under persecution. We name them: Moses, Joan of Arc, Martin Luther King. The point is that faith keeps us going even when promises are not being fulfilled. As Hebrews says, "These all died in faith, not having received what was promised, but having seen it and greeted it from afar" (11:13). And God has prepared for them and for us "the city which has foundations. whose builder and maker is God" (v. 10).

Faith is living amid unfulfilled promises with confidence in God's faithfulness to make good on His promises. Faith is living amid "uncertainties, Mysteries, doubts" with stability and serenity.[10] Faith is strength to go on when life has roughed us up. Faith is the determination to embark on a journey whose destination is known but not seen. Faith is working for God's righteousness and peace even when it looks like a losing battle. Faith is the blessed assurance that inexplicably sweeps over you and holds you up when everything crumbles around you.

Faith is the gift of a steadfast and faithful God whose steadfastness and faithfulness in relationship to us makes us steadfast and faithful.

When Pascal died, his family found a piece of paper sewed into the lining of his clothing. On it was his description of his conversion experience—the time he gambled his life in the wager of faith—and he had kept it on his body always. Here was what he wrote:

<blockquote>

The year of Grace, 1654
Monday, November 23rd
. . . .
Fire
God of Abraham, God of Isaac, God of Jacob.
Not of the Philosophers and the men of Science.
Certainty, Certainty, Feeling, Joy, Peace.
God of Jesus Christ

</blockquote>

Deum meum et Deum vestrum.
Thy God shall be my God.

. . . .

Joy, Joy, Joy, tears of Joy.[11]

Such was the gift of faith given to Pascal who took on the wager of faith. Would you like a little wager? I have the best one in the world. Faith in the God of Jesus Christ. It can make you whole.

### Notes

1. Blaise Pascal, *Pensees* (Chicago: *Great Books of the Western World*, Vol. 33, 1952), pp. 214-15.
2. *Wishful Thinking* (New York: Harper & Row, 1973), p. 20.
3. Flannery O'Connor, *The Habit of Being* (New York: Farrar, Straus, & Giroux, 1979), p. 350.
4. *Pensees*, pp. 222-23.
5. See *Wishful Thinking*, pp. 25-26.
6. Dietrich Bonhoeffer, *The Cost of Discipleship* (New York: The Macmillan Co., 1963) p. 54.
7. C. S. Lewis, *Mere Christianity* (New York: Macmillan Publishing Co., 1976), p. 123.
8. *Pensees*, pp. 215-16.
9. Reported in a letter by Flannery O'Connor, *The Habit of Being*, p. 164.
10. John Keats spoke of negative capability as our "being in uncertainties, mysteries, doubts, without any irritable reaching after fact and reason." *Selected Poems and Letters* ed. Douglas Bush (Boston: Houghton Mifflin Company, 1959), p. 261.
11. Pascal, *Thoughts*, selected and translated by Moritz Kaufmann (Cambridge, 1908), pp. 217-19.

MAY THE GOD OF HOPE FIL YOU WITH JOY AND PEACE IN BELIEVING SO THAT BY THE POWER OF THE HOLY SPIRIT, YOU MAY ABOUND IN HOPE

# 15
# Hope

There are few resources for living more essential than hope. Our survival as persons and the survival of our communities depends upon the presence of Hope. Without it, we give up and, whether or not our bodies are yet in the grave, die. A person without hope can see nothing good coming from the future; the alternatives have been narrowed to one bleak horizon dark as midnight. It is as if the whole bright circle of existence has closed to just a pinpoint of light, then disappeared. There may be nothing more painful to the human psyche than the loss of hope.

Similarly, communities that have lost any vision of a good future break apart and disintegrate.

"Where there is no vision, the people perish" (Prov. 29:18, KJV), says the wisdom of the Bible.

So it is that one of the great gifts of God is the gift of hope. It is God who gives us the power to hope. No wonder the apostle Paul placed it in the top three along with faith and love; and while love may be "the greatest of these" (1 Cor. 13:13), there is no virtue more distinctively part of the Judeo-Christian way of life than hope.

## I

Hope turns our faces toward the future because the biblical

God is a God of the future who lures us toward the promised fulfillment of the kingdom of God.

The kingdom of God, variously referred to as the messianic reign, the kingdom of Heaven, the new heaven and new earth, points to the promised completion of all existence: a reconciled humanity, a flowering earth, and a renewed communion with God. So we have been given wonderful images of the kingdom: Swords beaten into plowshares and spears into pruning hooks, springs flowing in the desert, wolf and lamb lying down together, nations becoming neighbors and neighbors becoming friends and friends becoming family, God walking with us and wiping away our tears saying, "Death shall be no more."

The biblical God comes from the future to give us power to hope in these things. Without such a vision we would despair and die.

A man who had a miserably unhappy marriage lost no time in immediately remarrying upon the death of his wife. Samuel Johnson remarked sardonically that it was "the triumph of hope over experience." Hope is always such a triumph. Hope announces that the future is not a repeat of the past, nor is it a continuation of the present; there is something new coming. The apostle Paul reasoned. "Now hope that is seen is not hope. For who hopes for what he sees? But if we hope for what we do not see, we wait for it with patience" (Rom. 8:24-25).

The triumph of hope over experience is manifest in the impoverished couple who bring children into the world hoping that the children's future can be better than theirs, and in the social reformer who keeps on trying to change society for the better even as injustice seems to reign, and in the person who despite devastating events in her life refuses to give up on life. Hope sets the Harlem congregation singing "I am bound for the promised land" or an East Tennessee mountain church singing "When we all get to heaven" or a Dixieland band marching down the street playing "When the saints go marching in" in a New Orleans funeral. As G. Temp Sparkman says, "Hoping is born in us when we stand at the mercy of the impermanent, the irrational, and the unjust. Hoping is set against the trauma and bewilderment of the transient, the absurd, the unjust.[1]

Hope invests the present with a meaning not justified by the circumstances of the present. With hope we can perceive, however faintly, an outline of meaning in the midst of tragic and broken existence. Pilgrims en route to America endured extraordinary hardships crossing the Atlantic because of their hope in a new life in the "New Land." In the Judeo-Christian perspective all God's people are pilgrims on the way toward the kingdom's Promised Land. With that we go on, no matter how difficult the path. The infusion of meaning which hope brings from the future into our present is an enormous resource for living. It gives us a spiritual/mental/emotional hardiness which helps us cope with the difficulties of the present.

## II

In the Bible, hope is represented by a cluster of words. Hope is trust in the God of hope who comes from the future to bring life. Hope is endurance during bad times, enabled by that hope. Hope is confident expectation (the opposite of dread) that God is on His way with a future brimming with goodness! Hope is waiting, waiting on God, patient, doggedly, persistent waiting, waiting as long as it takes for God to bring the fulfillment of His kingdom.

Just as there are multiple words in the Bible for hope, so also are there multiple images. Hope is walking in darkness searching for the light; it is enduring the silence of God waiting for His Word; it is sitting in chains, never giving up the dream of freedom; it is wandering in the wilderness looking for the Promised Land; it is facing your brokenness yearning to be made whole. Hope is acknowledging the absence of God while hungering and thirsting for His presence.

One of my favorite images of hope is Ezekiel's vision of the valley of dry bones. God showed Ezekiel a valley filled with skeletons. "Can these bones live?" God asked. Ezekiel mumbled his reply: "Only You know that." God then spoke to the bones, breathed into them His Spirit, and they came to life. The bones took on flesh, muscle, and skin, and as the spiritual goes, "The toe bone was connected to the foot bone" and so on until every skeleton in the valley was brought joyously to life. Then God explained the dream. "The bones are the whole house of Israel . . . they say, 'Our bones are dried up, and our hope is lost; we are clean cut off.' " God instructed Ezekiel to tell the people: "Thus says the Lord God . . . I will open your graves and raise you from your graves. . . . I will put my Spirit within you and you shall live!" (Ezek. 37:1-14).

Who of us has not felt like that valley of dry bones, all dried up, hope is lost, clean cut off. God's Spirit can bring us back to life.

Hope is represented most importantly by two great events, one the centerpiece of the Old Testament, the Exodus, and the other the centerpiece of the New Testament, Easter. The Exodus fills us with human historical hope: That God is at work in history to free those who are enslaved and work His miracle of life when all seems hopeless. God hears the cry of the oppressed and topples the pharaohs of the world. People of God become God's agents in delivering human historical hope to the poor of the earth. We do it by feeding the hungry, by becoming advocates of the oppressed and by opposing Pharaoh.

The Easter event sounds the trumpet call of resurrection: The best is not at the mercy of the worst. Death is not the final word, life is; hatred is not the final word, love is; the grave has not the final word, God does. The resurrection of Jesus Christ signals God's final victory over sin and death, a victory which spans this world and the next, opening up the gates of eternal life.

Resurrection hope sustains us in the face of our deaths and the deaths of those we love. In his profound and moving book *To Live with Hope* Temp Sparkman tells of his first trip back to Louisville after he and his family moved to Kansas City. He went to visit the grave of his daughter, Laura Suzanna, who as a child had recently died from leukemia. He writes:

My first trip back to Louisville was in late October, when the area was graced with autumn's artistry and ambience. Autumn's painting, inspiring in its beauty, could not hold back the melancholy. I celebrated the beauty, as in years past, but needed no encouragement to be pensive, for Laura Suzanna's grave lay before me. Kneeling, I rubbed my fingers across the etchings on the gravestone, perhaps unconsciously searching for some brailled cosmic words to heal the pain. I cried and waited in silence. At first hearing only memories, my ears were suddenly tuned to the October breeze, which hitherto had not been apparent. It filtered gently through the trees, carrying and rustling the falling and fallen leaves. Against an unaccountable chill over me, I pulled my sweater tighter about, for in the hush the wind carried Easter stirrings.[2]

## III

What we must not forget about hope is that God is the source of that hope and its object.

God, the source of hope, gives us the power to hope. It is a gift from beyond our present experience. In the New Testament hope is always a noun, *hope,* never an adjective, *hopeful,* or an adverb, *hopefully;* for it is far more than some subjective feeling we conjure up. It is a power given us by God, the God of our hope.

God is not only source but also object of our hope. We hope "in the Lord," not in princes or professors or priests, not in human power or human knowledge or human goodness. Neither do we believe in some vague notion "that everything will turn out all right." While we do affirm with Paul "That in everything God works for good with those who love him, who are called according to his purpose" (Rom. 8:28), we do not say it glibly, for we know that we ourselves may never see the good being worked out, at least not now, and never completely in this life. We hope for what we do not see.

## IV

This brings us to a consideration of a necessary companion virtue to hope: patience.[3] Impatient people cannot wait for God to bring in the kingdom in His good time and in His way, but rather insist that it happen now, by whatever means available. Hope and patience need each other. Hope without patience turns either to fanaticism or to despair. Patience without hope turns either to complacency or to cynicism.

Hope believes in the future perfection of the self and completion of existence, but without patience it demands that the fulfillment come now. Such impatience can lead to despair, as the political activism of the flower children of the 1960s quickly turned to despair when their protests did not quickly usher in the new society. Impatient hope can also lead to fanaticism. We are tempted to adopt violent or coercive means in our desire to accomplish the goals of the kingdom. All God's children yearn for justice, that the hungry be fed, the abandoned cared for, the oppressed set free. When our passion adopts violent means we have fallen into fanaticism. Being willing to die for God easily turns into being willing to kill for God.

Communism is an example of hope without patience. Violent, totalitarian means are used to secure the goals of justice. But there is no true justice without freedom. As Henry Kissinger put it, the most crucial issue facing the nations of the world is whether they can be just and free.

But as hope needs patience, so patience needs hope. Without a burning hope for a better world patience turns to complacency and settles for the world as it is, or it becomes cynical and says that world can never be any better, so grab what you can.

The intersection of hope and patience teaches us the proper relationship of means and ends. Hope without patience says "The end justifies the means." The folly of that philosophy is easily documented in America the past twenty years. In contrast, the biblical Christian says, "No, the end does not justify the means. Our means are to be as pure as our ends. Our means are themselves a realized presence of the kingdom of God in history." People of patient hope use means as pure as their ends trusting God to use these means to accomplish His good, just, and perfect end.

So, we cannot kill for the sake of the kingdom, we cannot coerce people into believing, and we cannot sacrifice individuals for the sake of the whole. To adopt violent or coercive means reveals that we have stopped trusting God to bring in His kingdom in His time and in His way.

## V

There is a hero of hope I would hole up before you: Martin Luther King, Jr. He is an exemplar of hope in these ways: (1) He was filled with God's dream to make this world more like the kingdom of God; (2) He adopted means consistent with the kingdom of God, a nonviolent resistence; (3) His vision of a final victory beyond the grave gave him uncommon bravery in the face of death.

A Baptist preacher's son, Martin grew up with dreams of God's kingdom dancing in his head. In the face of enormous injustice he dreamed God's dream of a "Beloved community," a land free from injustice, poverty, and racism, where his children and all children would not be "judged by the color of their skin but by the content of their character."[4] When Rosa Parks was denied a seat on a Montgomery bus, King led a boycott which gave great hope to all the underclasses of American society. He could not pray "Thy kingdom come on earth as it is in heaven" without giving God some help toward that end and giving people hope that God's kingdom could come a little nearer.

As fervent as King's hope in the kingdom was, however, he refused to force its arrival through violent means. The means he chose were consistent with Jesus' teaching on love: a nonviolent resistance. His resistance to unjust laws proved his hope; his nonviolent form of resistance proved his patience.

Finally, King's hope in the victory of God's kingdom gave him astonishing bravery in the face of death. Every day he received death threats, every march he risked physical beating or the assassin's bullet. But God had led him up a mountain and he had taken a look.

And I've *seen* the Promised Land. And I may not get there with you. But I want you to know tonight that we as a people *will* get to the Promised Land. So I'm happy tonight. I'm not worried about *anything*. I'm not fearing *any* man. Mine eyes have seen the glory of the coming of the Lord. I have a dream this afternoon that the brotherhood of man will become a reality. With this faith I will go out and carve a tunnel of hope from a mountain of despair. . . . With this faith, *we* will be able to achieve this new day, when all of God's children—black men and white men, Jews and Gentiles, Protestants and Catholics—will be able to join hands and sing with the Negroes in the spiritual of old, "Free at last! Free at least! [six] Thank God almighty we are free at last.[5]

In all this he was a follower of Jesus Christ, Hope of our hope, who preached the kingdom of God, who laid down His life for our sakes and the sake of that kingdom and whose resurrection opened heaven's door not only for Him but for all of earth's children.

### Notes

1.  G. Temp Sparkman, *To Live with Hope* (Valley Forge: Judson Press, 1985), p. 14.

2.  Sparkman, pp. 105-106.

3.  I am indebted to Stanley Hauerwas for his guidance in this connection. See his *A Community of Character* (Notre Dame: University of Notre Dame Press, 1983), pp. 102-106.

4.  From *Let the Trumpet Sound* by Stephen B. Oates (New York: Harper & Row, 1982), p. 486.

5.  From his famous "I Have A Dream" speech and his last address before his death.

SEE
WHAT
LOVE THE
FATHER
HAS GIVEN
LOVE US.
AS IF FROM
ANOTHER
THAT COUNTRY,
WE
SHOULD BE CALLED
CHILDREN
OF GOD AND
INDEED
WE
ARE.

# 16
# Love

We conclude this journey through the land of sins and virtues with love. Love is properly the one at the "end" in both meanings of the word: end as the conclusion and the end as the fulfillment. For love is the meaning and the end of all virtue and without love none of the virtues are true virtues.

*Wisdom* without love is a tedious and self-serving sophistry; it is cleverness in the pursuit of any ends, a cleverness without conscience; it is a dangerous technocracy. Paul Tillich rightly warns that we should distrust every claim for truth where we do not see truth united with love.[1]

*Courage* without love is rashness; it is mindless zealotry; it is a rebel without a cause or with too mean a cause. A person who is willing to die for truth might be willing to kill for truth —unless that person also has love.

*Justice* without love is at best the balance of power and at worst vindictive retribution. Reinhold Niebuhr was right: "Any justice which is only justice soon degenerates into something less than justice. It must be saved by something which is more than justice."[2] That something more is love.

*Temperance* without love turns into a grim-faced asceticism, a loveless renunciation of this world's gifts, or into a manic athleticism, a self-help regimen of diet and exercise— and love of God and neighbor go wanting.

And as for faith and hope? The apostle Paul was right: However great they are "the greatest of these is love," and without love, faith and hope are less than the real thing (1 Cor. 13:13). How can we have faith or keep faith in a God whom we cannot love? And who hopes for what one cannot love? Without love, faith can grow proud and dogmatic; without love, hope can grow fanatical.

Love is the meaning and end of all virtue and of all the virtues, and, as we discovered in the chapters on the sins, the seven deadly sins are all distortions of Love. As Dante illustrated in the *Divine Comedy,* pride, envy, and anger are perverted love (we take delight in what should grieve us); sloth is a deficiency of love; greed, gluttony, and lust are excessive love. Sin is a distortion of love itself—just as Satan is pictured as a fallen angel.

So it is important that we now focus on love.

# I

Love is sweet. Who can forget the sweetness (not unmixed with terror) of first falling in love. The love of a friend is a healing balm. Some of us have been so gloriously loved by our parents during the years of nurture that no matter how difficult our growing up days and adult days we have always, every minute of the day felt loved. We bask in love as in the first warm rays of summer sun. We come to life as we are loved by another. There is new spring in our step, new blush to our complexion, new sparkle in our eyes. Nothing is so life-affirming, so creative in its power, as love. When the large collection of "Helga" paintings were recently unveiled by Andrew Wyeth, reporters flocked to Wyeth's wife to ask what all these paintings of a neighboring woman were about. Betsy Wyeth gave a one word answer: Love. And she meant something far deeper than the sensation-seeking minds of the reporters would grasp. Love is the creative source of all art and all life. Love is sweet.

The second admission is this: We are bad at love. Nothing seems more important than to love and to be loved, but we feel that whenever God passed out the instructions on how to love, we were someplace else.

Some of us are fools for love, rushing recklessly into one bad relationship after another. Or, we're beggars for love. There is no moment when the empty place in us yearning for love gets filled. For whatever reasons buried in our past, we have an enormous deficit of love. Never have we felt completely, fully loved, and our hands are ever reaching, reaching, chasing away those whose love we most desperately want. Or, we are bumblers at love, always stuttering and tripping over our feet in the presence of those we adore. We so want the intimacy of knowing and being known, but when we try to communicate it's like we're speaking a foreign language—*parlez vous francais?* We feel we never quite connect with another person. We are the sad clown at the circus trying to love without words, but the feet are too big and the gestures cannot quite mime out the message. A tear runs down the white face.

Sometimes we feel like fakes at love, pretending to be selfless in our love when in fact our giving of love is but a ruse to get love back. Our devouring need to be loved determines everything.

Some of us are scared of love. We don't think people will love us if they really get to know us, so we hide. Others of us are Don Juans; we seduce others with our charm but never make commitments; we go from one person to another, discarding lovers like disposable wrappers.

So we're bad at love. Let's just say at love we're all amateurs —which isn't so bad a word since *amateur* comes from the Latin word "to love" and refers to a person who does something for the love of it. That's how all of us want to be loved—for the love of it. Who wants professional love?

Love is a mystery. A five-year-old boy in my congregation spied an attractive blonde-haired college student in the choir and after the concert went up to her and exclaimed, "You're so beautiful I could scream with love." That expresses love's fascination and its fear, its ecstasy and agony.

Love is something we never master. We are amateurs at it all our lives. We are like the procession of acts on "Ted Mack's Amateur Hour." We're not quite on key, our dance steps are not quite secure, but we're singing our hearts out and dancing the best we can, all for the love of it, till we get it right.

## II

This chapter is about how to get better at love, and immediately we run into problems. What exactly is love? How do we define it? There is no word used and abused more than this one. We use it to get love or to coerce a partner for our lust. We use it to control people we, in fact, dislike. If definitions elude us, slogans have ruined the word: "America, Love It or Leave It"; "Make Love Not War"; "Love Means Never Having to Say You're Sorry."

Part of the problem is that English language has only one word for *love*. The Greek language has four: *epithemia* (desire, close to lust), *eros* (love of the beautiful, true, and good), *philia* (brotherly/sisterly friendship love), and *agape* (the love of God, a self-giving love). Nygren reduces the four to two, *eros* and *agape*.[3] Reinhold Niebuhr divided love into two—mutual love and sacrificial love.[4] C. S. Lewis differentiated "need love" from "gift love." Henry Fairlie posited his grouping of four: dependent love, reliant love, bestowing love, and disinterested love.[5] Where do we begin? I agree with Buechner:

> The first stage is to believe that there is only one kind of love. The middle stage is to believe that there are many kinds of love and that the Greeks had a different word for each of them. The last stage is to believe that there is only one kind of love.[6]

Finally all love is one: The love of God with all your heart, mind, soul, and strength and the love of neighbor as yourself. Love of God, love of others, and love of self all have their origin in God's love given to us: "We love because he first loved us" (1 John 4:19). There are better and worse ways to love, more and less healthy ways to love, wise and unwise loves, but all love is one: The giving of the self to God and to others that communion and community might happen.

## III

How do we learn this love and how do we get better at it? The answer is this: As we become part of the biblical story and enter the stream of God's love and power. "Love has a history,' wrote Daniel Day Williams, and he was referring to God's history with us revealed in Jewish and Christian Scriptures and continuing with the church's history into our own histories.

As we enter into this history of love, we discover love's true meaning, and more, we are given power to love.

Love's history begins at creation where we discover that God's creation of us was itself an act of love. When God made the rest of creation He looked and said, "That's good": When he made the human race, he said even more. He said, "That's me!"[8] It is like the wonder of a parent who first sees his or her newborn child and says, "That's me, that baby is flesh of my flesh, bone of my bone!" Scripture says that God made us *in His image* which is the capacity for love, the will to be in communion with another.[9] We are not only part of a good creation, we are God's children. As I John says, "See what love the Father has given us—love as if from another country—that we should be called children of God; and indeed we are" (3:1).[10]

Some scientists today, called sociobiologists, are hypothesizing that from our creation the *homo sapien* species has had an altruistic gene. We have survived as a species because we have been created to care for others. Rene Dubos argues as a scientist for the goodness of humankind from the discovery of a prehistoric skeleton of a congenitally crippled and blind person of older age. The implication is that even before civilization and culture *homo sapiens* had a caring sense that nourished into old age a helpless member of the tribe.[11] So (the psychiatrist, psychoanalyst, philosopher) Willard Gaylin challenges the pessimistic tone of twentieth-century sciences with this affirmation: "Man cares because it is his nature to care. Man survives because he cares and is cared for. . . . Civilization is, at least in part, a form of crystallized love."[12]

To be sure, the image of God in us has been distorted in our world and by our world. The theological term for this disfigurement of God's image in us has been called *the fall*. We have chosen not to love and the result has been alienation and estrangement. Neo-Freudian Erich Fromm has his own psychoanalytic version of "the fall": We have lost our natural capacity of love, like an animal who no longer has the impulse, but must relearn love as an art.[13]

The history of love does not stop at "the fall." It pictures a God who throughout history has tried to lure us back to the way of love, a God who stayed faithful to us even though we were unfaithful to Him. The Old Testament calls this character of God *hesed*, the covenant love, steadfast love of God—the stubborn, patient, persistent, never giving up, no-matter-what love of God. God decided to commit Himself unconditionally to us. He determined in His heart to do whatever He had to do, to give whatever He had to give in order that His creation might flourish.

## IV

The supreme manifestation of God's love was through the life and death of Jesus of Nazareth. The sending of this His son was itself an extraordinary gift of love—to loose the son you love into a world that will do Him harm is beyond our human heart's capacity to comprehend. This Jesus showed God's love for us. This Jesus reconnected us with the divine image within us for He was "the image of the invisible God" (Col. 1:15), and when we looked at Him we saw truly who God is and who we are. Jesus was more than a clearer definition of love; when we stand before Jesus we stand before Love itself.

By looking at Jesus we see the character of true love. Jesus' love was characterized by a number of things. First, an impartial goodness extended to all people, both good and bad. Jesus welcomed all people, even sinners, into His company. The good, religious folk accused Him of being a friend of prostitutes, tax-collectors, and sinners. They meant it as an insult; He took it as a compliment. That He became a scandal to "good" people was indeed tragic, for they didn't recognize His love for them too, not until it was too late, not until they heard Him say with dying breath on the cross, "Father, forgive them, for they know not what they do" (Luke 23:34). And they realized He was praying for them, forgiving *them*.

Second, Jesus' love was characterized by an astonishing forgiveness. Jesus' acceptance and forgiveness knew no bounds except the bounds we placed at the doors of our hearts. This forgiveness flowed to us even before speeches of repentance parted our lips—and still does.

Third, this love was characterized by sacrificial self-giving. His was an extravagant love, not counting the cost. Self-giving love is the way of human fulfillment, as Jesus put it, "He who finds his life will lose it, and he who loses his life for my sake will find it" (Matt. 10:39). This is the riddle of existence: As we give ourselves away in love, we find ourselves. Contemporary psycho-wisdom tells us that we cannot love others until we love ourselves. Jesus tells us that we learn to love ourselves as we love others, and the beginning of this love is God. God's history of love provides what our personal histories have failed to supply. We love because God first loved us. The world's slogan is "self-realization through self-acceptance." Jesus' way is "self-acceptance through self-giving."[14]

Some new research is confirming Jesus' riddle. David McClelland has documented the elevation of the immune system's ability to fight upper respiratory infection in those who regularly spend an hour with a friend reminiscing about people who they have loved and who have loved them. Also, people who viewed a Mother Teresa film experienced a quanitifiable temporary rise in immunological capacity. A Harvard graduate student, James McKay, has found that people who have fantasies of selfless love report fewer infections and their T-cells (lymphocyte disease fighting cells) show greater resistance to virus.[15] Jesus was not selling self-giving love as some patent medicine to cure whatever ails you, but He was suggesting that you live better, you live healthier and happier, when you give yourself to others.

Fourth, Jesus' love was an aggressive, initiative-taking love that went out to people and bestowed worth. Love does that: It bestows worth. When someone you love displays love for you, your very being is enhanced. Love is creative; it builds up the other. Jesus' love bestowed worth on people who were discarded by society—women, children, racially mixed Samaritans, sinners—and His love lifted them up.

Fifth, Jesus reminded us that love is a command. Love is the basis of all the commandments. Jesus summarized the whole love of God in this double command: "You shall love the Lord your God with all your heart, and with all your soul, and with all your mind. . . . You shall love your neighbor as yourself" (Matt. 22:37-40). At its base, love is a command addressed to our will. We are not commanded to like our enemy but to love our enemy, and this means we act in goodwill toward them. I like the way Theron D. Price expressed it: "This love which comes to us as gift and sustenance remains with us as demand. If it may sometimes be ecstatic vision, always it is moral vocation. It sacrifices more than it glows."[16]

Followers of Jesus find that their love begins to follow the form of Jesus' love. It is characterized by: (1) a generosity of spirit which wants the good of all people; (2) a forgiving spirit which no longer allows the past to be an impediment to communion and community; (3) a self-giving spirit which does nto count the cost or calculate the return; (4) an enhancing love which bestows worth; and (5) the determination of the will to act in goodwill toward others, even the enemy, the one who tempts you to return evil for evil.

You may feel overwhelmed by the demands of that kind of love; it may seem so far beyond you. Do not despair. When the history of love becomes our history, when we follow the Christ into that history, we discover the mystery of the Christian life:

Christ comes to dwell in us and His spirit gives us the power to love. "God's love has been poured into our hearts through the Holy Spirit," Paul expresses (Rom. 5:5).

## V

In closing there is one companion virtue to love that is a wonderful, if forgotten virtue: steadfastness. It is the human derivative of God's *hesed*, His steadfast love. It is the combination of faith, hope, and love for it is faithful, hopeful, and loving, all three. It means fidelity in the covenant-love of marriage; it means faithfulness to friends; and it means commitment to community.

Our society has all but destroyed this virtue. People are disposable. Serial marriage replaces lifelong monogamy. Friendships are as fragile as one disagreement. Community is nearly impossible in our society; we are taught an individualism which denies the richness of community, and upward mobility has made us all transient passers through.

The reason the church believes in lifelong monogamy, in long-lasting friendships, and in durable community is that these things best reflect the character of God, His steadfast, forgiving, never-giving-up love.

So we people of love say, we don't give up on people, we don't get rid of people, we stick with each other through good times and bad, riches and poverty, sickness and health. In the 1960s, Joni Mitchell sang a song about people searching "for love that sticks around." By God's grace we have found such a love (and been found by it); by God's grace, the power of Christ in us, we can live such a love.

You may have failed at such love, but do not despair. For your past, God's grace always comes as forgiveness; for your future, God's grace comes as power to meet the goal.

## Notes

1. Paul Tillich, *The New Being* (New York: Charles Scribner's Sons, 1955), p. 74.

2. Reinhold Niebuhr, *Moral Men and Immoral Society* (New York: Charles Scribner's Sons, 1932), p. 258.

3. Anders Nygren, *Agape and Eros* (London: S.P.C.K., 1953).

4. Reinhold Niebuhr, *The Nature and Destiny of Man* (New York: Charles Scribner's Sons, 1941), Vol. II, Chapter 3.

5. Henry Fairlie, pp. 191-214.

6. Frederick Buechner, *Wishful Thinking* p. 53.

7. Daniel Day Williams, *The Spirit and the Forms of Love* (New York: Harper & Row, 1968), pp. 1-15.

8. The paraphrase/interpretation of Fred Craddock recorded in lecture.

9. Williams, The imago dei definition is a cornerstone of Williams' systematic theology centered on love.

10. The translation of 1 John 3:1 by George Arthur Buttrick, recovered from private conversation.

11. Willard Gaylin, *Caring* (New York: Alfred A. Knopf, 1976), p. 44.

12. Ibid., p. 13. This caring sense, argues Gaylin, is engendered and demanded in the extended helplessness of the human infant.

13. Erich Fromm, *The Art of Loving* (New York: Bentom Books, Harper & Row, 1956).

14. Paul Lehmann, *Ethnics in a Christian Context* (New York: Harper & Row, 1963), p. 16.

15. Louisville *Courier-Journal*, July 29, 1986, pp. B7&8.

16. Theron D. Price, in a pamphlet form of addresses on "Faith, Hope, and Love" delivered to the Furman University faculty.